THE
SEYCHELLES

THE SEYCHELLES

Unquiet Islands

Marcus Franda

Westview Press • Boulder, Colorado

Gower • Hampshire, England

Profiles/Nations of Contemporary Africa

Published in 1982 in the United States of America by
  Westview Press, Inc.
  5500 Central Avenue
  Boulder, Colorado 80301
  Frederick A. Praeger, President and Publisher

Published in 1982 in Great Britain by
  Gower Publishing Company, Ltd.
  Gower House
  Croft Road
  Aldershot, Hants., GU11 3HR

Library of Congress Catalog Card Number 82-1979
ISBN (U.S.) 0-86531-266-4
ISBN (U.K.) 0-566-00552-2

Printed and bound in the United States of America

To Stephanie

Pour qu'elle comprenne

Contents

Tables and Illustrations

Tables

Illustrations

Preface

This book was written between November 1978 and June 1981 as part of my coverage of the Indian Ocean area for Universities Field Staff International (UFSI). Formerly the American Universities Field Staff, UFSI is a consortium established in 1951 of eighteen universities, research institutes, and other educational organizations.[1] The presidents of the universities that founded the Field Staff felt the need for a career corps of area-based scholarly journalists who could report to Americans on contemporary affairs around the world. With its change of name in 1981, the present leadership of the Field Staff has dramatically set forth its aspirations to expand the organization to include non-U.S. associates and universities and to report to a global rather than a U.S. audience.

The Field Staff espouses no causes, promotes no ideology, aligns with no political group, has no governmental connections, and favors no particular social science theory. As a Field Staff associate since 1971, my principal charge has been to write readable and balanced short articles (called Field Staff Reports) on events of significance for a predominantly U.S. audience. The Field Staff also publishes a journal called *Common Ground*, makes educational films, prepares television documentaries, and hosts conferences. It is funded in part by the eighteen educational institutions that sponsor it, in part by the sale of its books, articles, films, and television programs, and in part by grants from foundations, private corporations, and individuals interested in the study of world affairs.

Special mention of appreciation for getting me started on this book must go to Drs. Lloyd Lewan and John Tymitz of the Institute for Shipboard Education, who first introduced me physically to the Seychelles, and to Dr. Larry W. Bowman of the University of Connecticut, who suggested I write the book. Lewan and Tymitz got me through the stormy seas of the Indian Ocean – on occasion, even without boilers – while Bowman guided this enterprise through the stormier climate of university life in the United States. I am especially grateful to the Field Staff for funding the research on which this book is based and for allowing me to publish it in the Profiles/Nations of Contemporary Africa series of Westview Press. Lynne Rienner, Jeanne Remington, and Susan McRory of Westview Press deserve praise for their excellent work.

My family—Vonnie, Charlie, and Stephanie—have earned more tributes than I can pay them for their help in collecting data and writing. They ran errands for me, took pictures, edited manuscripts, and provided the warmest camaraderie and companionship that a father and husband could hope for. By now they understand the foibles of a cantankerous writer better than anyone else in the world. Mrs. Soundara Raghavan of the American Institute of Indian Studies in New Delhi merits special mention for typing this and most of my other manuscripts over the past few years.

There are many other people in the Seychelles—in the government, in the party, in the army, and elsewhere—whom I would like to thank, but I hesitate to do so because mention of their names could cause some of them difficulties. They will recognize the thoughts, materials, and discussions they so generously shared with me reflected in the pages that follow. My hope is that the book will exhibit the balanced judgment and accurate use of data their contributions deserve. Errors of judgment and fact should be ascribed entirely to me.

It should be pointed out that, despite their failings, the present party and government contain large numbers of people who are enthusiastic about the experimental enterprises in which they are engaged, are open about their plans and methods of proceeding, and have been candid with me about their failings. Because of these people, Seychelles does not yet have a government like so many others in Africa and Asia that have been lost entirely in machinations to stay in power. It is still possible for a foreign journalist or scholar to move about in society and discuss important issues.

My personal hope is that the government will shift further in the direction of greater openness while maintaining the dedication and hard work that have been exhibited by its young and vibrant members and adapting its programs to realities when it recognizes clear failures. In that event, it could have an outside chance of legitimizing the very brutal methods it used to come to power and remain there. It would certainly be an appropriate future scenario for a set of idyllic islands whose motto has been for more than a century, *Finis Coronat Opus*.

Turtle Bay, Mahé   *Marcus Franda*
Seychelles

NOTES

1. Members of the consortium are the University of Alabama at Birmingham, University of Alabama at Tuscaloosa, Brown University, California State University at Fullerton, California State University at Northridge, Dartmouth College, East-West Center, University of Hawaii, Indiana University, Institute for Shipboard Education, University of Kansas, University of Malaya, Michigan State University, University of Missouri, University of Pittsburgh, Ramapo College of New Jersey, Utah State University, and the University of Wisconsin system.

1

History

The Republic of Seychelles is one of the tiniest nations in the world. The total area of all its lands is no more than 171 square miles (444 square kilometers), about one and a half times the size of Martha's Vineyard in Massachusetts. According to the 1977 census, the population of the entire country was 61,898, slightly less than Kalamazoo, Michigan, or Troy, New York. Like many other small countries, Seychelles has a romantic appeal, particularly to those who value the intimacy and individualism usually associated with small geographical size, but the islands are being challenged by a number of problems resulting from their past parochialism and their diminutive world stature.

How can a tiny country like Seychelles survive economically? Where can it mobilize the human and other resources to make itself viable in a world of rapid change? How can it preserve its distinctive national identity and cultural values? Is it possible to maintain anything resembling its past peacefulness and unspoilt beauty? What is to prevent it from being overwhelmed by the massive world forces of the late twentieth and early twenty-first centuries?

These questions are perhaps felt a bit more intensely in Seychelles than in other small territories because the country was historically far more isolated than other lilliputian states and yet now finds itself in the midst of a destabilized ocean area of considerable strategic importance. Completely uninhabited until two hundred years ago, and then only sparsely populated by ex-slaves, European adventurers, and Asian traders, the country was suddenly opened up to major influences from the great powers with the building of a U.S. satellite tracking station in the 1960s and construction of a first-rate international airport in 1971. A massive boom in international tourism has since proceeded apace with conflicts over conservation, fishing rights, and oil exploration. Strategic and commercial factors have stimulated the interests of, among others, the Soviet Union, China, France, India, Tanzania, Kenya, and the United States, as well as a number of Arabs and South Africans. The coup d'etat that took place on 5 June 1977, and the abortive coup attempt of

1

November 1981 are only indications of the turbulence that stirs beneath the calm and breathtaking beauty of this idyllic group of islands.

PHYSICAL FEATURES

There are ninety-two named islands in the Republic of Seychelles, plus a number of smaller unnamed bits and pieces.[1] These islands are geographically located in four major clusters—commonly called the Seychelles, Amirante, Farquhar, and Aldabra groups—with four small solitary islands (Denis, Bird, Platte, and Coetivy) having been included in the country along with these four main groups because of their proximity. The largest of the islands in terms of land area are Mahé, Praslin, Silhouette, Aldabra, and Cosmoledo, but 97 percent of the population lives on only three islands (Mahé, Praslin, and La Digue). Only these three islands and Silhouette have enough people to have schools. The distance between Mahé, the major island, and Aldabra, the most remote, is more than 700 miles (1,100 kilometers). With 200-mile (320-kilometer) zones of economic rights around each of its islands, the government of Seychelles estimates that it has jurisdiction over some 400,000 square miles (1 million square kilometers) of the Indian Ocean, more than any nation other than France and India (see Figure 1.1).

Unlike other islands in the Indian Ocean, forty-two of the Seychelles islands are geologically distinguished by the fact that they are granitic rather than coralline or volcanic. Recent theories of plate tectonics and continental drift—developed in part by international Indian Ocean expeditions in which scientists from Wood's Hole, Scripps, the Smithsonian and other U.S. institutions participated in the 1960s—have lent credence to the theory that the Seychelles were once, millions of years ago, part of a massive continent known as Gondwanaland, in which India and Africa may have been joined. According to this theory, the Seychelles represent "a continental fragment left during the widening of the Indian Ocean."[2]

Theories of continental drift have been bolstered by the fact that the granitic islands of the Seychelles are among the few granitic oceanic islands in the entire world, a freak of nature that produces a truly unusual and breathtaking landscape. Massive granite mountains and peaks rise dramatically from long coastal beaches; exposed rock surfaces have been beaten and pounded by the surf into a beautiful assortment of shapes and textures. The highest peak on any of the islands is Morne Seychellois, on the main island of Mahé, which towers 2,990 feet (920 meters) above sea level, but all the granitic islands have surprisingly rugged small mountains or peaks that boom up from the ocean and the sand. Although there are no large rivers in the Seychelles, numerous mountain streams and waterfalls cascade down rocky slopes, fed almost daily by a bountiful rainfall, varying on the average between 50 and 120 inches (130–300 centimeters) per year from the driest to the wettest islands.

As the Seychelles lie only 4° to 11° south of the equator, they are distinctly tropical, but the climate of the islands is moderated considerably by the calm seas that surround them. As the noted botanist Jonathan Sauer has put it, the equatorial, oceanic climate of the Seychelles has an "unearthly mildness."[3] All the islands, with one or two minor exceptions, lie outside any cyclone or hurricane belt. They are influenced primarily by trade winds that tend to blow from the southeast during the months of April to October and from the northwest during May to November. Average wind speeds are only 10 to 18 knots per hour, depending on the time of year, which means that a damaging storm is an exceedingly rare event (the only known hurricane to strike any of the inhabited islands occurred in 1863). The northwest winds bring rains that are known as the monsoons, but they are also so tame as to seldom cause any damage. Actual rainfall is rather evenly spread throughout the year (it usually rains a bit every second or third day, with rare exceptions) so that relative humidity is always quite high (75 percent or more all year round). Temperatures seldom fall below 70°F (21°C) and never rise above 90°F (32°C) even on the hottest day of the year. Light and constant cool breezes from the sea tend to make the climate idyllic throughout the year and at any time of day.

The coralline islands are quite different from the granitic islands in several important respects. They were originally formed by the activities of a small sea animal called the coral polyp, which usually anchored itself onto some of the rocks or mountain peaks below the ocean's surface and then sucked in seawater as a means of extracting the nutrients with which it built coral reefs. All the Seychelles islands have many coral reefs off their coastlines, but fifty of the largest coral accumulations have themselves become named islands. The coralline islands are remarkably flat, rising barely a few feet above sea level, and none of them are nearly so lush and teeming with vegetation as the granitic group. Few of the coralline islands have any permanent population because they lack drinkable water; those that do have settlers have only a handful. The largest coral island is Aldabra—one of the largest atolls in the world—which is essentially a massive lagoon encircled by coral land barriers. Aldabra itself is 22 miles (35 kilometers) long and 8 miles (13 kilometers) wide; its lagoon is almost large enough to contain every one of the islands of the Seychelles if placed side by side.

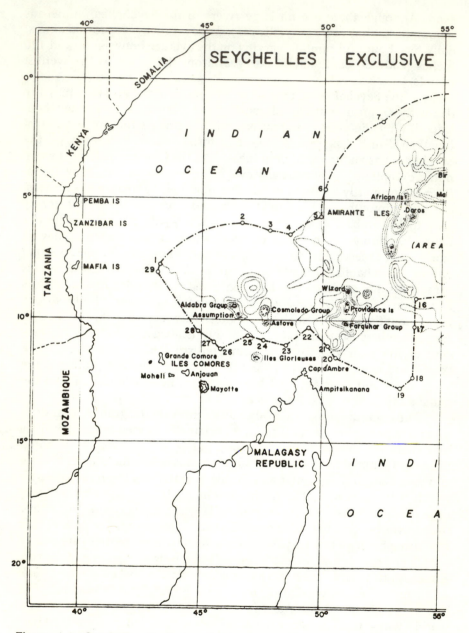

Figure 1.1. Seychelles Exclusive Economic Maritime Zone. Map drawn by Ministry of Works and Port, Survey Division, government of Seychelles, Victoria, Mahé, and published in the 5 June 1978 issue of *The Nation*, Seychelles' only daily newspaper. Published by permission.

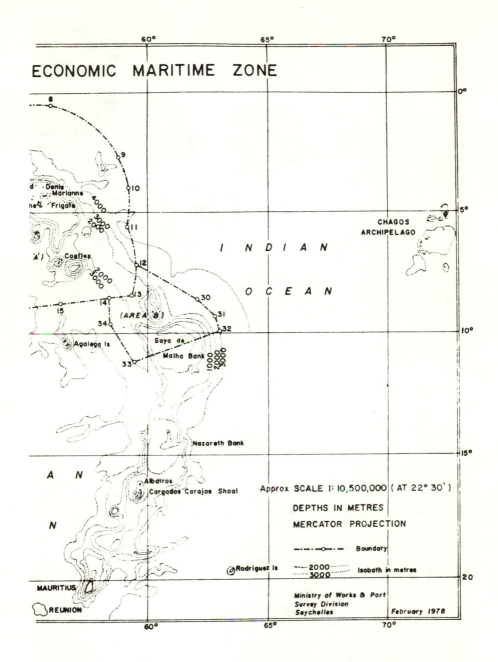

ECONOMIC MARITIME ZONE

CHAGOS ARCHIPELAGO

I N D I A N

O C E A N

d ·Denis
·Marianne
he ·Frigate

4000

3000

'A') Costlev

2000
3000

13
15   14
(AREA 'B')
34

30
31
32

Agalega Is

Saya de
Malha Bank

1000
2000

33

Nazareth Bank

A N

N

Albatros
Cargados Carajos Shoal

Approx SCALE 1: 10,500,000 (AT 22° 30')

DEPTHS IN METRES

MERCATOR PROJECTION

Rodriguez Is

Boundary

2000
3000   Isobath in metres

MAURITIUS

REUNION

Ministry of Works & Port
Survey Division
Seychelles   February 1978

Figure 1.2. A view of one of the thousands of wide and unspoiled beaches on the islands. Author's photo.

EARLY EXPLORATION

It is primarily the distance of the Seychelles fragments from other land masses – Mahé, the main island, is 980 miles (1,568 kilometers) from Mauritius, 1,748 miles (2,800 kilometers) southwest of Bombay, 990 miles (1,584 kilometers) east of Mombasa, and 1,410 miles (2,256 kilometers) south of Aden – that produced the extremely isolated conditions in which the islands existed until recently. Isolation was also encouraged because the routes of pre-European seafarers on the Indian Ocean – Arabs, Persians, Indians, and Chinese – followed a monsoon arc that brought them up the coast of Africa and then across to India, far to the west and north of the Seychelles.[4] There are old Arabic manuscripts (dated 810 and 916 A.D.) describing voyages to islands that sound remarkably like the Seychelles, and marks resembling Arab inscriptions have been found on rocks on Frigate and North islands, both in the Seychelles group. A.W.T. Webb, one of the most reliable historians of the Seychelles, speculated that Polynesians "from some place around the Bay of Bengal" may have stopped on the Seychelles in 200–300 B.C. on their way to Madagascar, where they eventually settled.[5]

Despite these early hints of human contact, however, it is clear that the first permanent human settlement on any of the islands took place in

1771, when fifteen "blancs" (whites) and seven slaves, along with a slave commander named Miguel, five South Indians, and a Negress, came from Mauritius and Réunion, settling first on St. Anne and later on Mahé. Those who immediately followed these first settlers were either Frenchmen who had fled France when revolution threatened, Frenchmen who had quit India earlier when the French had failed there, or, in far greater numbers, African slaves accompanying their masters. In most instances the white men in the new colonies were trying to make or recoup fortunes by establishing a new trade in tortoises and timber. By 1789 it was estimated that more than 13,000 giant Galapagos-type tortoises had already been shipped out from Mahé, and the population of the colony had grown to 591 people (of whom 487 were slaves). In the nineteenth and twentieth centuries a number of British people—primarily from India, Rhodesia (Zimbabwe), Kenya, and other former British colonies—settled in the Seychelles, either to retire or for commercial purposes, but this influx was surprisingly small considering that the British had ruled the colony for more than a century and a half.

The earliest settlers in the Seychelles did not denude the environment, but they did alter it considerably and rapidly. Before they arrived, hundreds and thousands of years of tropical growth, unmolested by man, had produced a rare ecological wonder, sometimes described as the last truly virgin territory in the world. The first well-documented description of the Seychelles archipelago was by an English expedition known as the Fourth Voyage of the East India Company, which visited Mahé, North Island, and Silhouette in January 1609. An Englishman from that expedition, John Jourdain, then described dense black forests with floors of guano a foot deep and a wealth of sea and bird life. Jourdain's description of the area around what is now the main port of Victoria is as follows:

> . . . there is as good tymber as ever I sawe of length and bignes, and a very firme timber. You shall have many trees of 60 and 70 feete without sprigge except at the topp, very bigge and straight as an arrowe. It is a very good refreshing place for wood, water, cooker nutts, fish and fowle, without any feare or danger, except the allagartes [alligators], for you cannot discerne that ever any people had bene there before us.[6]

Perhaps the first Europeans to discover the Seychelles were the Portuguese, who explored a number of the islands around Mahé between 1501 and 1530 and named them the Seven Sisters (Sête Irmanas). Both Vasco da Gama and Sebastian Cabot were among the early explorers who visited some of the islands and made charts, and there was a small Dutch settlement that reportedly struggled along on some of the smaller islands from 1598 to 1712. From the time of Jourdain's visit until the first permanent settlements, the Seychelles provided refuge for a number of pirates and privateers.

The most legendary of all Seychelles pirates was Olivier le Vasseur, better known as "La Buze" (the buzzard), who in the 1720s joined with another pirate, John Taylor, and terrorized French and British shipping in the Indian Ocean. Le Vasseur was captured by the French and hanged on 7 July 1730, but just as he mounted the scaffold he is reported to have thrown a piece of paper at the crowd and yelled: "My treasure to he who can understand!"[7] The paper contained a map and a cryptogram, copies of which still exist. From 1948 to 1970 a man named Reginald Cruise-Wilkens spent a small fortune in funds collected from speculators, trying (in vain) to find the Buzzard's treasure on the north coast of Mahé, in a honeycomb of man-made tunnels that may or may not have been constructed by Le Vasseur.

The first Americans to become involved in the Seychelles were a group of successful pirates who operated in the Indian Ocean in the late eighteenth century. The most noted of these was Captain Nemesis, a man born on Pimlico Sound in Carolina Colony who went to England and bought himself a commission in the Royal Navy in the mid-eighteenth century.[8] In 1762 Nemesis was cashiered on a charge of theft and deported to Australia, but he led a mutiny en route to Australia, took over the ship, and eventually acquired a pirate fleet of fifteen vessels, many of which were based in the Seychelles. A number of historians have reported that Nemesis enjoyed considerable success in part because he was quietly respected and encouraged by the French—because he reserved most of his hatred for the British.

American merchants from Salem and New Bedford, Massachusetts, tried to open up an extensive Indian Ocean trade in the 1780s by selling salted cod to Madagascar in exchange for zebu, the Malagasy cattle. In 1782 Americans constructed an abattoir in Morondava (Mauritius) where zebu were slaughtered, salted, dried, and loaded as beef jerky for eventual sale in the United States and South America. George Davidson reported that 197 ships of U.S. registry were logged in the books at Port Louis (Mauritius) between 1797 and 1810, at a time when Port Louis was a free port. Most of these ships belonged to U.S. privateers buying goods from Mauritian pirates who had in turn robbed them from British ships returning from India. Such practices were helped along by Secretary of State James Monroe's dictum on "freedom of the high seas," but they were eventually stopped by a British blockade of Mauritius and by French patrols operating out of the French island of Réunion. Davidson, in fact, argued that the French captured Réunion initially in order to have a base from which to counter Mauritian pirates and U.S. privateers.[9]

Had American merchants been more persistent in the Indian Ocean, the history of the Seychelles might have been quite different. As it was, however, the Seychelles were influenced exclusively by France and Britain. The most successful Americans in the Seychelles in the nineteenth century were whalers who would put out from Salem or New Bedford or Cape Cod for two to three years at a time. U.S. whalers could be found, in Davidson's words, "from Kerguelan to the Sea of Okhotsk, from Cape Horn to the Persian Gulf," operating ships that were remarkably small for the job at hand.[10] Lacking ship space, the whalers would turn blubber into whale oil at small interim bases in areas of major activity; one such base (for seventy years) was on St. Anne Island in the Seychelles.

The heyday of the whalers was the middle of the nineteenth century, the last U.S. ship coming to St. Anne in 1904. U.S. mercants in the nineteenth century eventually decided not to go into the Indian Ocean in a big way because the China trade opened up across the Pacific and both the Atlantic and the Pacific supplied enough activity to keep Americans occupied. In the Indian Ocean, until recently, the Americans subordinated their interests to those of the British. Perhaps the epitaph of the early American trade was written by a chronicler in the *Seychelles Annual Report* of 1904, who recorded that "these islands contain a number of Americans and Portuguese from Cape Verde, who had been left behind from whalers, and most of whom are handy, hard-working settlers."

FRENCH AND BRITISH RIVALRY

The Seychelles were first charted extensively by France in the 1740s, at the instigation of Bertrand François Mahé de La Bourdonnais, then governor of Mauritius and Réunion (or Ile de France and Bourbon, as they were known then).[11] La Bourdonnais had decided that, if there was to be another war with Britain, he would be well advised to explore the uncharted and unnamed islands north of Madagascar so that France might have a more direct route to India. La Bourdonnais sent out major expeditions to the Seychelles in 1742 and 1744; the leader of these two expeditions (Lazare Picault) reciprocated La Bourdonnais's patronage by naming the major Seychelles islands Iles de la Bourdonnais. Shortly thereafter, however, La Bourdonnais became involved in a series of naval battles with the British in India, eventually capturing Madras, and this ended his mapping and charting activities in the Seychelles. The jealousy and rivalry between La Bourdonnais and Joseph Dupleix, governor-general of the French East India Company in India, eventually resulted in the downfall of La Bourdonnais and his execution at the Bastille. In 1756, when the French Crown assumed direct control of Ile de La Bourdonnais, the name of the colony was changed to Séchelles, after a French controller general of finance, Vicomte Moreau de Séchelles (the spelling was later changed officially to "Seychelles" when the British took over the islands in 1814).

The Seychelles were first claimed by the French in 1756, when an expedition led by Nicholas Morphey planted a "stone of possession," bearing the arms of France and the date, on Mahé at an impressive ceremony on 1 November 1756. It was in this era that individual islands in the vicinity of Mahé acquired their present names, many of which were the names of French ministers (Praslin), ships (La Digue and Cerf), or officials (Silhouette and Desroches). It was also in this era (beginning in 1771) that the islands were first colonized, the initial impetus for colonization coming from French administrators on Mauritius who thought that settlers on the Seychelles might be able to plant spices outside the cyclone belt in quantities sufficient to compete with the growing Dutch monopoly of the spice trade. The original settlers—from Mauritius and Réunion—did bring cinnamon, cloves, nutmeg, and other spices with them, but they soon abandoned spice growing and the spice trade for the more lucrative trade in tortoises and timber. Spices are now grown and exported from the Seychelles, but their development took place long after the establishment of the first colony.

An attempt by the first settlers to declare their independence from both Mauritius and France in 1789 was put down by two French commandants of long tenure, who guided the colony through the stormy years of the French Revolution and the Napoleonic Wars. The first of these was Jean Baptiste Philogene de Malavois, whose training in engineering, agronomy, and geography enabled him to build defense and administrative establishments and to set about regulating land occupation. Prior to Malavois, land had been occupied and cleared in a chaotic manner, with no authority able to establish individual rights to the forests, the coconut groves, or the shoreline. Visitors in the 1770s reported that English ships were repeatedly raiding some of the islands and that the colonists were "hunting turtles instead of cultivating crops, perishing from hunger at each others' throats, [allowing] deserters from the garrison to burn the forests while stealing slaves, [and allowing] runaway slaves to ravage newly planted fruit, spice and sugarcane plantations."[12]

Malavois instituted an orderly land tenure, which conceded to each "habitant" (free colonist) an area of 108 arpents (112 acres, or 45 hectares) fronting on the coast, and to freed slaves an area of 27 arpents (28 acres, or 11 hectares) each. This original division has continued to influence landholding patterns up to the present day, as have a number of other policies established by Malavois. One of the most important aspects of the original land division was that much of the land area was reserved for future colonists. A key proposal of Malavois, that cutting of timber for export be strictly controlled and cleared land replanted with selected species, was for the most part insufficiently adhered to until recently.

The successor to Malavois as commandant was Chevalier Jean Baptiste Quéau de Quinssy, a shrewd and adaptable aristocrat who took charge of the colony for thirty-three years. Prior to his long tenure in the Seychelles, Quinssy had been assigned to the royal household in Paris and had served as a captain in the Regiment of Pondicherry in India. Quinssy governed the Seychelles in the name of France until 1815, when he changed his name to Quincy and became the first British administrator of the islands (he died in 1827 at the age of 79). Until the British firmly established their rule with the Treaty of Paris in 1814, Quinssy found it necessary on seven occasions to run up the Union Jack when British ships were sighted coming into port, only to replace it with the French Tricolor after the British had left. At one point Quinssy even had a blue and white cloth flag prepared, on which were sewn the words "Seychelles – Capitulation."

Quinssy built a thriving shipbuilding and shipping industry and a diversified plantation system along lines proposed by Malavois. Both shipping and the plantations were based on the labor of slaves from Africa and Madagascar. They were supplemented by the development of fishing and turtling and by the growing of local crops (rice, maize, millet, manioc, sweet potatoes, bananas) and animals (pigs, fowl, cattle, and sheep), all of which had been brought in from the outside during these early years of settlement. By the mid-nineteenth century most of the original cover on the main islands of the Seychelles had been replaced by a thriving new imported plant life.

The amount of native timber taken out of the Seychelles during Quinssy's thirty-three years is often exaggerated, but it is clear that many millions of feet of fine woods were cut for export and shipbuilding in the late eighteenth and early nineteenth centuries. Auguste Toussaint, the noted French historian of the Indian Ocean, has scoured calendars and gazettes, declarations of shipmasters, and customs records to estimate the extent of the Seychelles shipbuilding industry, and he has concluded that native timbers were used to build at least one hundred big ships, most of which were sold in Mauritius.[13] The largest Seychelles-built ship was the 372-ton (335–metric ton) *Thomas Blyth*, built in the 1820s for the English merchant James Blyth, who named it after his father and made it the first of a fleet of fifty merchant ships. The *Thomas Blyth* was one of the few Seychelles-built ships ever to cross the Atlantic; most of them were built specifically for trade among India, Madagascar, and Australia. Blyth's ships were particularly distinctive because they were painted a

Figure 1.3. Chevalier Jean Baptiste Quéau de Quinssy (1748–1827), Governor of the Seychelles for 33 years. Photo courtesy of the Carnegie Museum and Library, Victoria.

shade of yellow green, which led most people to call them "the pea-soupers."

Timbering and the plantation system introduced by Quinssy took their toll on the ancient forests of Mahé and its surrounding islands. By 1819 a knowledgeable visitor to the Seychelles (M. Frappas) reported that most of Mahé, Praslin, La Digue, and Silhouette islands had been stripped of their original wooded cover and many other islands had been conceded to plantation owners but not yet fully occupied. In the nineteenth and twentieth centuries, the plantation system has been fully developed, with many islands being conceded in toto to individual owners for use as a plantation and many other huge plantations being delineated on the larger islands. A predominantly plantation economy has survived until the present day, despite the assumption of power in

1977 by a genuinely socialist government, largely because the domestic and export economies of the Seychelles have been very heavily based on the products of the plantations.

Although French culture has continued to influence the Seychelles for the last two centuries, French rule was never well established. Until they relinquished control of the colony to the British in 1810, the French considered the Seychelles to be a peripheral dependency of Mauritius, of value primarily as a convenient place to dock and repair ships or freshen up sailors.[14] Some of the original settlers tried to gain their independence from the French in June 1790 by setting up a Permanent Colonial Assembly and a Committee of Administration and repudiating all links with Mauritius, but this mini-manifestation of the French Revolution was put down with the arrival of a Republican commandant on the islands in late 1790. In 1791 a French attempt to abolish slavery without compensation was defeated by a colonists' boycott of the proclamation. It was not until the 1830s, when the British were willing to use coercion on a much larger scale than the French, that slavery was effectively abolished in the Seychelles.[15]

A series of naval confrontations between the French and British in the Seychelles began on 16 May 1794 with the appearance off Mahé of an English squadron of five warships, carrying more than 1,200 men and 162 guns. All inhabitants of Mahé were convened by gunshots fired at four-minute intervals, but bloodshed was avoided when Quinssy capitulated to the British and negotiated a treaty protecting the colonists, their slaves, and their property. When an 1802 treaty (the Peace of Amiens) failed, Napoleon decided to station a strong fleet on the main trade route to India, with Mauritius as its naval and military headquarters, Réunion and Madagascar as depots of food and stores, and the Seychelles as an advanced outpost. The British response was to place a naval blockade on all these islands, resulting in six more capitulations by Quinssy over the next six years.[16] During these years, the Seychelles prospered under the terms of Quinssy's capitulation agreements, which brought many ships of both France and Britain to Mahé.

THE BRITISH COLONIAL PERIOD

The British fought for Mauritius and the Seychelles because Mauritius commanded the route between India and the Cape and because French corsairs and pirates were a menace to British East India Company ships returning from India. Britain assumed control over Mauritius during the course of the Napoleonic Wars, in 1810, but the actual transfer of Mauritius and the Seychelles to the British was not formalized until the Treaty of Paris in 1814. Part of the agreements of capitulation, which were negotiated for the Seychelles in large part by Quinssy, stipulated that the British would respect the French settlers on the Seychelles, as well as the French language and French customs.

Although the British were eager to put a stop to French interference with shipping lanes to and from India, they did not particularly want to assume the responsibility of governing either Mauritius or the Seychelles. British diplomats had tried to trade the Seychelles and Mauritius for France's possessions in India at the Treaty of Paris in 1814, but the French had refused. The Seychelles, therefore, were rather indirectly and reluctantly ruled by the British until 1903, being technically a dependency of Mauritius, which was in turn a full-fledged British colony. In 1903 the Seychelles were granted the status of a British crown colony in their own right, but most Seychellois quickly indicated that they would have preferred to remain under indirect rule. On 22 October 1921 a group of influential Seychellois addressed a public petition to London, praying for the reamalgamation of the Seychelles with Mauritius on grounds of poverty. The petition was ultimately rejected by the British secretary of state for the colonies.[17]

The political history of the Seychelles in the nineteenth century consists essentially of a series of constitutional steps upgrading the status of the colony.[18] Its affairs were managed by a British agent from Mauritius until 1839 and from then until 1872 by a civil commissioner. From 1872 until 1889 political power was gradually broadened to a British Board of Civil Commissioners resident in the islands; in 1889 nominated Executive and Legislative Councils were established that finally included some Seychellois citizens. A full-fledged governor, charged with the responsibility of administratively separating the territory from Mauritius, was assigned to the Seychelles for the first time in 1897. Separation was accomplished on 31 August 1903. From that date until Independence Day in 1976, the only remaining link between Mauritius and the Seychelles was through the judiciary, as the Seychelles' court of appeal for civil cases remained in Port Louis.

Twentieth-century politics prior to independence reflected the increasing Seychelloisation of government and the extension of the franchise.[19] Elected representation was introduced into the Legislative Council in 1948, when approximately 2,000 citizens were declared eligible to vote (on the basis of literacy and property qualifications) for four members of the twelve-member council. The nature of the franchise meant that only the landed strata of Seychelles citizens were represented in the legislature, with the result that the Seychelles Taxpayers' and Producers' Association (STPA) easily won all seats at all elections prior to 1963. Political participation then expanded rapidly with the formation of two major political parties in 1963 and the introduction of universal adult franchise in 1967.

In the 1967 elections, the Seychelles Democratic party (SDP), led by James Mancham (pronounced man-kam), won four of eight elected seats, with the Seychelles People's United party (SPUP) of France Albert René winning three seats and the eighth seat going to an independent.[20] From that point forward the STPA ceased to be a factor in Seychelles politics. Both Mancham and René pressed the British for the establishment of a Westminster system of government, with René originally adopting a more militant posture in favor of complete independence. The result was a new constitution and new elections in 1970, in which Mancham's SDP won ten seats and René's SPUP, five. As a consequence of that election, Mancham became the first chief minister of the Seychelles. He continued to be the chief executive of the colony until its independence in 1976 and ruled as its first elected president until 5 June 1977 when he was overthrown in a coup d'etat that was masterminded by René. Many observers attribute Mancham's downfall to his inclusion of René in a coalition government after the 1974 elections, in which Mancham's SDP won thirteen of fifteen seats in the Assembly with only 52.4 percent of the vote.

Conflicts between Mancham and René in the 1960s and 1970s reflected a series of contradictions that had developed during the period of British rule. Mancham was inclined to the view that capitalism and colonial status were acceptable to most Seychellois so long as Seychellois leaders were allowed to run their own economy and make their own decisions. René emphasized immediate independence, "socialism," and other "progressive" measures as the only effective way to deal with the problems of poverty and British neglect. As John Ostheimer has pointed out, the SPUP was always divided on questions relating to the meaning of socialism and the extent to which it should be tied to African liberation movements.[21] Ostheimer also described both Mancham and René as being essentially motivated "by desires to have access to political machinery through which they could press their claims to a part of the prosperity that seemed about to dawn in emergent Seychelles."[22]

Burton Benedict, an anthropologist who is one of the most astute and sensitive observers of Seychellois society, has attributed the Seychelles' historic poverty to ineffectual government by both the French and the British and to the exceedingly poor state of communications between the Seychelles and the rest of the world.[23] Prior to 1903 all commerce was channeled through agents in Mauritius, who charged freight rates that were greater than the prevailing rates between England and Mauritius. The Seychelles administration was often forced to order supplies from England through Mauritius without knowing what they would cost until the items appeared in the accounts of funds owed to Mauritius by Seychelles. The first savings bank in the Seychelles appeared only in 1874, and the first commercial bank was set up as late as 1959! Under such circumstances, it is little wonder that Seychelles had to develop in relative isolation during the course of its colonial history.

By 1830 the population of the Seychelles had grown to a temporary peak of just over 10,000, of whom more than 9,000 were slaves. In these early years, exports were almost entirely timber, tortoises, and sea turtles, with turtle shell, salt fish, fish oil, and coconut oil being subsidiary export commodities. The first recorded export crop was cotton, which appeared initially as an item of trade in 1796, became the main export for a quarter century after 1802, and at one point accounted for almost half the cultivated area on Mahé. Cotton gave way to sugarcane as the principal export in 1831, when international cotton markets came to be dominated by the United States. Sugarcane started giving way rapidly to less labor-intensive coconut plantations with the abolition of slavery in 1834.

Since the 1840s the coconut has reigned supreme as the principal export commodity of the Seychelles, although there have been some changes in processing of the crop. Prior to the twentieth century, coconut oil was the main export, but oil has now been replaced by copra. Copra is the dried white fleshy interior of the coconut, which can be pressed as a source of vegetable oil and used in the manufacture of soap, margarine, and cooking oil, but Seychelles copra is of such high quality that it is usually consumed as a delicacy rather than processed further. In the first half of the twentieth century, copra was shipped primarily to Europe; since 1951 most of the Seychelles copra has gone first to India and now to Pakistan. Sauer estimated that 40–50 million coconuts were grown in the Seychelles every year in the 1960s, with nearly 90 percent of total production being converted to exports. A recent survey estimated that total production in 1978 was down to only 20 million coconuts, the decline stemming from incidence of the *Melittomma* beetle on some plantations and general neglect on others. Personal consumption of coconuts has declined, on the average, from 150 nuts per year in the 1960s to 32 nuts per year in the 1980s.[24]

The shift from cotton and sugarcane plantations to coconut plantations was essentially the result of the abolition of slavery in 1834. Census records indicate that the population fell from 8,500 in 1830 to 4,360 in 1840, primarily because many settlers left with their slaves—for territories where slavery was legally permissible—rather than remain in the Seychelles and submit to the new British laws. Most of those settlers who remained then switched to growing coconuts instead of maize, rice, cot-

Figure 1.4. Copra production, Seychelles style. Coconuts are simply split in half and dried. Seychelles government photo.

ton, vegetables, and sugarcane, with the result that "never since then has Seychelles been able to provide enough food to feed itself."[25] Ironically enough, the population of the Seychelles jumped dramatically in the next few decades, largely because the islands became a dumping ground for slaves freed in other colonies. Indeed, the population more than tripled in the forty years following 1840 – growing to 14,191 by 1881 – before it was slowed again by two smallpox epidemics in 1887 and 1895.

Most of the slaves who came to the Seychelles early came directly from Mauritius, but large numbers of them had simply been on Mauritius after having been taken from Mozambique, Madagascar, Somalia, and East Africa. After the Emancipation Act of 1834, and in spite of treaties with Britain and the sultan of Zanzibar that banned the slave trade, Arab traders continued to traffic in slaves in the Indian Ocean. In order to stop this illicit trade, the British navy began in the 1860s to patrol the East African coast, chasing dhows and other slave ships and releasing slaves. Most of these liberated slaves were freed in Mombasa, but some were released in Aden and still others in Bombay or the Seychelles. In the museum and archives in Victoria there is a "liberation register" that lists the names and sex of many of the freed slaves who were brought to the Seychelles in the late nineteenth century.

Once in the Seychelles, most of the freed slaves were taken care of by missionaries, who established homes for them, converted them to Christianity, and educated their children. Some of the older slaves were employed as plantation laborers or as domestics, often under conditions of employment that were not too different from what they had known before. To a greater extent than is true in almost any other part of the world, however, slaves or the children of slaves in the Seychelles have intermarried with the nonslave population, producing a variety of racial types that defies the imagination of people from societies without much miscegenation. By 1901 the Seychelles census stated flatly that "it is no longer possible to distinguish the descendants of the African slaves from the other sections of the community."[26]

In addition to French and British settlers and ex-slaves, the Seychelles have been populated by several dozen Indian and Chinese families, most of whom are involved in commercial ventures.[27] A few Indians were among these in the earliest settlements, one of whom—a South Indian named Ramalingam—received a very large land grant from the French. Most of the Indians in the Seychelles today trace their ancestry to a migration of Indian merchants from Bombay, Gujarat, and Kutch in the 1880s and 1890s, when the British started encouraging Indian merchants as a means of opening up the Seychelles to the outside world. Some few Indian Seychellois trace their origins to an earlier migration from Mauritius in the 1850s or to a later migration from South Africa in the twentieth century.

The first Chinese Seychellois came from Mauritius during the same two decades as most Indian merchants, but there was a small subsequent influx of Chinese traders from mainland China in the beginning of this century. The vast bulk of the Chinese in the Seychelles are from Canton, although the Chinese have tended to intermarry with other social groups to such an extent that the present generation of Chinese ancestry does not always have clearly identifiable Sinic features. Although the Indians have tended to marry and mate outside their community with less frequency than the Chinese (something that was possible because they could get brides and grooms with relative ease from nearby India), they have interacted with the rest of the Seychelles population to a much greater degree than is true of Indian communities in other parts of the world. As Kantilal Jivan Shah has pointed out, "the Indians are part and parcel of the Seychelles because their children today do not speak any Indian language . . . they speak only Seychellois Creole, French and English." Shah, who is perhaps the foremost scholar on the island, and whose son, Nirmal Jivan Shah, is fast following in his father's footsteps, is convinced that the Indian community is "being integrated into Seychellois society."[28]

Aside from those who migrated voluntarily to the Seychelles, there have been a number of Africans and non-Africans who have come to the islands as political exiles. Among the most famous have been Prempeh, king of Asante, who spent more than two decades on the islands at the beginning of this century and left a number of progeny; the kabaka of Buganda; a minor king of Bunyora; Sultan Ali, a tribal ruler from Somaliland; a would-be sultan of Zanzibar, Sayid Khaled bin Bargash; Saad Zaghul Pasha of Egypt; and Ali bin Ahmed Fadh of Aden. In 1800, seventy French Jacobins accused of attempting the assassination of Napoleon were exiled to the Seychelles; from 1875 to 1895 the islands were the home of Abdullah Kahn, the sultan of Perak, and a number of his followers, all of whom had been exiled from the Malay Peninsula by the British. The British government brought indentured laborers from Madras for road construction in the 1890s but later rejected proposals to use islands in the Seychelles as concentration camps for Irish political prisoners and prisoners of the Boer War. Most recently, the Seychelles were a temporary exile for Archbishop Makarios of Cyprus in the 1950s.

TIES WITH AFRICA

With such a rich background of migrations inward, it is not unusual to find Seychellois with French and Portuguese grandfathers, Indian and African grandmothers, a British mother and Seychellois or Chinese father, or an infinite variety of other combinations. The significant influence of the British can be appreciated by the existence in virtually every home of a prominent portrait or statue of the queen, who is known throughout the islands as "la petite tante" (literally "small aunt"). The overwhelming cultural influence of the French can be seen from the fact that 90 percent of the present population is Catholic, with only 8 percent belonging to the Church of England (the remaining 2 percent is accounted for by Hindus, Muslims, Parsis, Seventh-Day Adventists — most of whom are South Indians — and members of the Bahai faith, but there are no temples or mosques on any of the islands). French influence is also obvious in family, street, and place names and in the use of the Napoleonic Code as the basis for civil law.

One of the great debates that has taken place about Seychelles is the question of the extent of its "Africanness," or, indeed, whether it should even be considered a part of Africa. Seychelles joined the Organization of African Unity (OAU) when it first became independent in 1976, and the René government is an enthusiastic member of OAU, having been dependent on Tanzanian troops to come to power in the coup d'etat of 1977. The previous government, which is still the only government ever to come to power in competitive party elections, was tied much more

closely to Britain and Europe. The leading political party in that government was very reluctant to champion independence from Britain; its
president, James Mancham, was fond of saying that "nationalism is often
just another form of racism." One of the major issues in Seychelles today
is posed by the government's attempts to tie the country irrevocably to
revolutionary black African and international socialist movements, often
at the expense of tourism, aid, investments, and commercial dealings
with the West.

A typical British view has always been that Seychelles is a place
"halfway to nowhere," which has lost its cultural underpinnings. This
stereotype was perhaps most blatantly articulated by Williams Travis, a
British adventurer, when discussing the Seychellois Creole language in a
popular book written in 1959. Travis was of the impression that the
Creole patois of the Seychelles

> has neither grammar nor syntax, and constitutes the colony's greatest single
> handicap, shutting its inhabitants off from general contact with the outside
> world. It is no value commercially and prevents many from emigrating to
> other countries where they might otherwise be employed. There is,
> moreover, a definite prejudice against English, and although it is taught in
> schools, family and local influences bear down upon the young people to
> forget and discard this essential skill. If it were indeed French that was
> spoken, there would be no grounds for criticism, but this creole tongue has
> no historical or cultural background, no possibilities of development, no
> literature and no value as a language at all.[29]

In contrast to this popular notion, a number of British officials and
scholars have insisted that Seychelles Creole does have African roots and
that links back to Africa are also evident in Seychellois music, food, and
witchcraft. The historian Webb, for example, argued that

> the vocabulary of [Seychelles] creole is undeniably based on 18th century
> French roots, mingled with Kafir, Malagassy, Bantu and Indian elements.
> But what some are beginning to believe is not yet generally appreciated in
> Seychelles, namely that Creole is something more than Pidgin French . . .
> the Creole spoken in Seychelles is not patois; it is a language in its own
> right. It is an honest, thorough and comprehensive reconstruction of
> French from its roots to suit African requirements and idiom. It contains
> within itself an African accommodation to Western civilization.[30]

Echoing Webb's speculation about language has been a frequently
stated notion that Christianity in the Seychelles has tenacious African
roots. This theory was developed in some detail by a British scientist,
F. D. Ommanney, in another popular book of the 1950s, as follows:

Disproportionately enormous churches occupy commanding positions around the [Seychelles] coast, and on all the islands huge white
crosses proclaim Christ to approaching vessels far out to sea. The year is
punctuated by elaborate religious holidays and festivals, and every Sunday
the whole population of every village goes to mass . . .

. . . yet something foreign and African seems to have crept into the
Christian religion of the people, for it is to the African's deep superstition
and love of magic, as also to his love of pomp and display, that the Church
makes its powerful appeal. Side by side with the religion of Christ a much
older and darker one still lingers. The old savage gods have not yet been
quite driven out. In shacks and cabins up the mountainside live old ghouls
who practice witchcraft. They do a trade in love philtres and magic charms
. . . believed in by a surprising number of people.[31]

As is the case with Creole, the African roots of witchcraft and magic
in the Seychelles have often been viewed with suspicion. A particularly
thoughtful American woman who lived for a number of years on Remire
Island in the Seychelles has expressed her doubts as follows:

That the blacks have managed to combine a very considerable
amount of low-power magic, white magic, herbal lore, and vague superstitions into their already satisfying elaborate Catholicism is often cited as
proof of their former beliefs showing through – showing through so
strongly that it is the one area where they may be said to have influenced
the Europeans themselves. But it is surprising how much the flavor of the
superstitions is more rural European than African, and the few practices of
black magic are all types to be found in a little book called *Le Petit Albert*,
written by a Frenchman but unfortunately burned to the last copy by a
rabid librarian.[32]

The extent to which Seychelles shares a common culture with
Africa will be one of many questions that recurs in the pages that follow.
Ultimately, however, many of these questions can be answered only
after much more research has been conducted into such areas as language, religion, and witchcraft, as well as diet and music. In the absence
of such research, what has been attempted in the following chapters is an
assessment of what is presently known about the social, political, and
economic lives of today's Seychellois. The concluding chapter seeks to
analyze a number of factors that will inevitably affect ties between the
Seychelles, other parts of Africa, and the rest of the world.

NOTES

1. The ninety-two named islands are listed in the 1976 and 1979 constitu-
tions of the Seychelles; the list is reproduced in the appendix to Maxime Fayon,

Geography of Seychelles, 2nd rev. ed. (Victoria: Ministry of Education and Culture, 1978). The government is revising the list to include more recently named islands.

2. M. Fayon, T. Jackson, and R. Clyde, *Atlas for Seychelles* (London: Macmillan, 1977), p. 13. Perhaps the best continuing research on the Indian Ocean is being done at the university in Réunion. See, for example, Lucien F. Montaggioni, *Recherches géologiques sur les complexes récifaux de l'archipel des Mascareignes (Ocean Indien Occidental)* [Geological research on the reef complexes of the Mascarenes (Western Indian Ocean)], 2 vols. (St. Denis, Réunion: Centre Universitaire de la Réunion, 1979).

3. Jonathan D. Sauer, *Plants and Man on the Seychelles Coast: A Study in Historical Biogeography* (Madison: University of Wisconsin Press, 1967), p. 3.

4. Norman N. Miller, "The Indian Ocean: Traditional Trade on a Smuggler's Sea," *American Universities Field Staff Reports* No. 7 (February 1980).

5. A.W.T. Webb, *Story of Seychelles,* 3rd rev. ed. (Victoria: Government Printing Office, 1966), p. 6.

6. Quoted in ibid., p. 12.

7. The story of Le Vasseur is traced in detail in Roy Norvil, *The Treasure Seeker's Treasury* (London: Hutchinson and Company, 1978), pp. 50–60.

8. This section is based largely on George Bindley Davidson, "American Trade in the Indian Ocean (1795–1815)," *Journal of the Seychelles Society,* No. 3 (December 1963), pp. 1–10.

9. Ibid., p. 7.

10. Ibid., p. 10.

11. The classic historical study is J. T. Bradley, *History of Seychelles,* 2 vols. (Victoria: Clarion Press, 1940). Another extremely valuable book of the same period is by an Anglican archdeacon, J.A.F. Ozanne, *Coconuts and Creoles* (London: Philip Allan and Company, 1936).

12. Sauer, *Plants and Man on the Seychelles Coast,* p. 19.

13. Auguste Toussaint, "Shipbuilding in Seychelles," *Journal of the Seychelles Society,* No. 5 (October 1966), pp. 29–40.

14. French history in Mauritius and the Seychelles is traced in Carol Wright, *Mauritius* (Harrisburg, Pa.: Stackpole Books, 1974). See also Mervyn Brown, *Madagascar Rediscovered: A History From Early Times to Independence* (London: Damien Tunnacliffe, 1978).

15. Burton Benedict, "Slavery and Indenture in Mauritius and Seychelles," in *Asian and African Systems of Slavery,* edited by James L. Watson (Oxford: Basil Blackwell, 1980), pp. 135–168.

16. For a detailed study see G. S. Graham, *Great Britain in the Indian Ocean: A Study of Maritime Enterprise 1810–1850* (Oxford: Clarendon Press, 1967).

17. Kantilal Jivan Shah, "Fragments of History," *Commerce* (Bombay), Special Independence of Seychelles Issue, Vol. 132, no. 3396 (June 26, 1976), p. 9.

18. These are traced in *Report of the Seychelles Constitutional Commission, 1970* (Victoria: Government of Seychelles, 1970).

19. A brief history of twentieth-century politics appears in T. V. Bulpin, *Islands in a Forgotten Sea* (Capetown: H. B. Timmins, 1958).

20. Election results for the Seychelles prior to independence are available in *The Seychelles Handbook* (Victoria: Government Printer, 1976).

21. John M. Ostheimer, "Independence Politics in the Seychelles," in *The Politics of the Western Indian Ocean Islands*, edited by John M. Ostheimer (New York: Praeger Publishers, 1975), pp. 171–172.

22. Ibid., p. 168.

23. Burton Benedict, *People of the Seychelles*, 3rd ed., Ministry of Overseas Development, Overseas Research Publication No. 14 (London: Her Majesty's Stationery Office, 1970), p. 13.

24. Compare Sauer, *Plants and Man on the Seychelles Coast*, pp. 27–28, with *Report on the 1978 Agriculture Survey* (Victoria: Government Printers, March 1980), p. 25.

25. Quoted in *1977 Census Report* (Victoria: Government Printing Office, April 1978), p. 3.

26. Quoted in ibid., p. 5.

27. An excellent analysis of these communities is Burton Benedict, "Family Firms and Firm Families: A Comparison of Indian, Chinese and Creole Firms in Seychelles," in *Entrepreneurs in Cultural Context*, edited by Sidney M. Greenfield, Arnold Strickon, and Robert T. Aubey (Albuquerque: University of New Mexico Press, 1979), pp. 305–326.

28. Shah, "Fragments of History," p. 17.

29. William Travis, *Beyond the Reefs* (London: George Allen and Unwin, 1959), p. 21.

30. Webb, *Story of Seychelles*, pp. 43–44.

31. F. D. Ommanney, *The Shoals of Capricorn* (New York: Longmans Green and Company, 1952), p. 169.

32. Wendy Day Veevers-Carter, *Island Home* (New York: Random House, 1970), p. 337.

2

People

The population of the Seychelles in mid-1981 was an estimated 65,000; it was growing at the rate of 2.1 percent per year.[1] The most crowded island by far is Mahé, which contains 88 percent of the population (57,307 people) and has a population density of 970 people per square mile (388 per square kilometer). The remaining granitic islands contain 11 percent of the population, with Praslin (4,647 people) and La Digue (1,970) being the most heavily populated of the islands after Mahé. At the other extreme, all of the coralline islands put together accounted for a mere 599 people in 1981, which gave them an average population density of only 7.5 people per square mile (3 per square kilometer).

DEMOGRAPHIC VARIABLES

Although the population of the Seychelles is small in terms of numbers, there is no question that the country has a looming population problem. Birthrates are still substantial—28.9 live births per thousand in 1980—while the death rate has steadily declined, to only 7 per thousand in 1980.[2] Significant improvements in medical treatment, public health, and housing have already led to a reduction in infant mortality over the past few years. More such improvements promise an even greater impact on population growth rates in the future. As more than half of the present population was born after 1960, and 49.5 percent of this youthful population is female, the number of women entering reproductive age groups each year for at least the rest of this century is almost certain to be maintained.[3]

Fertility rates in the Seychelles have not been high in comparison with those of most other African and Asian countries, but population growth has nevertheless been rather steady. This is so primarily because the country has never witnessed a war (although it did provide some soldiers for the Allies in both world wars) and the climate of the islands is among the healthiest in the world. These and other factors have resulted in exceptionally low death rates. The Seychelles do have mosquitoes but have never known a case of malaria. Rats, mice, and cockroaches abound, but there has never been a case of plague. Also unknown to the islands are such dreaded Asian and African scourges as cholera, schistosomiasis, encephalitis, yellow fever, and rabies. Leprosy, tuberculosis, and smallpox have existed on the islands at one time or another, but in recent years all three have been eradicated by public health measures. Life expectancy at birth in 1979 was estimated at 65 for men and 71 for women, both figures being more in line with European and American expectations than with those of Asia and Africa.[4]

Among the animal population there is no foot-and-mouth disease, no rinderpest, no brucellosis, no tuberculosis, and no duck virus. The absence of plants and animals that are poisonous or otherwise harmful to human beings has led many observers to label the Seychelles a "garden of Eden" or "paradise found." There are only two species of garden snakes on the islands, and neither is poisonous. There are no stinging nettles and no ferocious beasts. Sharks are plentiful in the waters surrounding the islands, but instances of shark attacks on humans are rare (the Seychellois say that sharks need not attack humans because they have plenty of fish to satisfy their appetites). Swift undercurrents are present on less than 10 percent of the beaches. There are occasional high winds (usually no stronger than 40 miles [64 kilometers] per hour) on some of the outer islands, but, as indicated earlier, the entire oceanic area of the Seychelles is remarkably free from hurricanes, cyclones, or other extreme storms.

The population problem is becoming particularly acute because the capacity of the islands to accommodate human communities is severely limited. More than forty of the islands are presently uninhabited, most of these being mere specks on a map, surrounded by thousands of miles of ocean. The vast bulk of the uninhabited islands are coralline and are, therefore, almost entirely lacking in fresh water supply or scope for domestic cultivation. Mahé, the main island, now has a population density greater than that of the Philippines, Kenya, or most African and Asian nations, while Praslin (270 people per square mile, or 108 per square kilometer) and La Digue (352 people per square mile, or 141 per square kilometer) are as densely populated as Mexico and Egypt respectively.

The Seychelles government is hoping to restrict population growth on Mahé, to retain some of the more unusual and beautiful islands as unpeopled conservation havens or tourist resorts, and to maintain the rustic nature of La Digue (again, for reasons having to do with tourism) by severely curtailing population expansion there.[5] Large-scale population growth is planned for Praslin and some of the outer islands, with

Figure 2.1. Young Seychellois women at a government-sponsored youth function. Seychelles government photo.

hopes that rainwater and a few recently discovered underground aquifers can sustain both domestic settlements and modern agriculture. Provision of electricity to Praslin (which started only in June 1981) has already meant the felling of large numbers of old trees, a measure that could exacerbate existing erosion problems on that island and has certainly impaired its beauty. More than one-half the total area of the Seychelles consists of forestland, sand, coral, mountains, or boulders; only 10 percent of all land is arable, and only 2,160 acres (900 hectares) is considered suitable for agriculture.[6]

Population pressures are being felt most severely in the areas of housing, education, employment, and services. Although Seychelles still does not have the kind of grinding and degrading poverty one finds in India or much of Africa, this is so essentially because the climate is benign, the islands have been isolated from major epidemics and diseases, and both fish and coconuts have been plentiful. Projections for a population of 100,000 people or more by the year 2000 have left planners wondering whether Seychelles will be able to maintain anything resembling its present state of health and beauty. Almost certainly, the main island of

Figure 2.2. Seychellois sitting in front of the Post Office. There is a casualness about Seychellois life that is appealing to some, but is viewed as idleness by others. Author's photo.

Mahé will have to become more densely populated and urbanized than it is, as has happened to such beautiful places as Hawaii and Bali over the last two or three decades. There is some scope for increased food supplies through the development of a more intensive and efficient agriculture – and through systematic exploitation of the vast riches of the sea – but most observers agree that the Seychellois will be hard pressed over the next two decades to absorb ever-increasing numbers of people without despoiling the environment, altering the ecology, or lowering living standards.

On the positive side, the birthrate has come down from a high of 32.1 per thousand in 1974 to 28.9 per thousand in 1980, with the number of births each year remaining below the all-time high of 1,860 in 1974.[7] Declining fertility has thus far counteracted the increased numbers of women of childbearing age so that the number of persons of each age group up to 19 shows little variation (for example, it was estimated in 1980 that 19-year-olds just barely outnumbered 3-year-olds). The significance of declining fertility can be appreciated from the fact that census officials have revised downward – from 106,000 to 100,000 – their 1977 projections of the population for the year 2000, essentially because of the persistence of a declining trend in the birthrate.[8] Nevertheless, it is only from the age of 20 upward that the number of persons of each age group drops quickly, to only 679 persons aged 29 in 1980. This drop also reflects increases in the number of births during the 1950s, there being twice as many people aged 15–19 as there are in the age group 25–29.

Extensive use of contraceptives and widespread knowledge about birth control and the effects of excess population promise to reduce overall population growth rates at an accelerating pace. A study conducted in 1980 indicated that 33 percent of all Seychellois women in reproductive age groups (ages 15–49) were using some form of contraception.[9] Although this figure might not be impressive in a European context, it is larger than comparable figures in most of Asia and Africa and it does represent a substantial increase over the past decade. For a predominantly Catholic nation, it is considered quite unusual.

Family planning and population education programs are significantly aided in Seychelles by a literacy rate of more than 60 percent and by the fact that 95 percent of the population eligible for the primary grades is attending school. The most serious aspect of the present population boom is the addition of an expected 1,600 new entrants into the labor force annually during the next few years. This has already created widespread fear of unemployment and is the major reason for opening the country to tourism on a large scale. Compared to that in other parts of Asia and Africa, the employment situation in Seychelles is enviable, but the only reason for this is that tourism has absorbed large numbers of youths in meaningful jobs since 1971.[10]

RELIGIOUS BELIEFS

Declining birthrates in a country that is 90 percent Roman Catholic is only one indication that the Seychellois are quite independent where matters of religion are concerned. The Catholic church owes its present dominant position to the fact that the earliest white settlers in the Seychelles were Catholics and remained Catholics despite 162 years of British rule. Catholic church leaders still claim that the large-scale exodus of colonists from the Seychelles in the 1830s was due to an official attempt to force Protestantism on them, but Webb insisted that the exodus was related more to slavery economics and that the most concerted attempt to force Protestantism on the French came in the 1840s.[11]

From 1814 to 1853 the Church of England could conceivably have made gains in converting some of the population, as there were no Catholic priests living on the islands and the British colonial government was perfectly willing to provide patronage to Protestant missionaries. One reason for the failure of Protestantism was the obvious lack of interest in this faraway colony on the part of Anglican church leaders, the first Anglican civil chaplain (the Reverend G. T. Delafontaine) being named only in 1843. Even more important, however, was the identification in the minds of Seychellois of Catholicism with high status. To both upper and lower classes in the Seychelles, speaking French, practicing Catholicism, and having light-colored skin strengthened one's associations with the first free settlers and, therefore, all three came to be identified as signs of good pedigree. Moreover, Church of England leaders argued that the lower classes often expressed a love for the pageantry of the Roman Catholic Church, rejecting out of hand the "dour religious services of the Anglicans."[12]

The Church of England is presently supported by 8 percent of the population of the Seychelles, its largest following being on the island of Praslin, where 24 percent of the people are Anglicans. Preference for the Church of England has been declining in this century, Anglicans having accounted for 14 percent of the population in 1901. Most of the Anglican families were originally converted by missionaries in the latter half of the nineteenth and early twentieth centuries; Catholicism spread among the general population much earlier when slaves and ex-slaves tried to emulate and adopt the religion of their French masters.

Prior to 1853 the only Catholic priests on the islands were a few occasional visitors from Mauritius, with the result that facilities for legal and religious recognition of marriage and other rites of passage were lacking for more than three-quarters of a century. Because the early French settlers had to maintain their own churches and religious ceremonies without assistance from Rome or the bishopric in Mauritius, they often either demanded large amounts from their slaves and ex-slaves for the performance of ceremonies or refused them permission to marry without large donations to the church. One consequence of this early history was the establishment of a tradition of customary unions among Africans, who "complained of not having enough money to marry and of difficulty in securing their employer's permission."[13] As is discussed later in this chapter, the tradition of living "en ménage" has continued to the present day and is still flourishing.

The most serious attempt to impose Protestantism in the Seychelles came in the late 1840s, when Civil Commissioner R. W. Keate refused to allow a Roman Catholic priest to be based permanently in the islands because, in his words, this would be "wilfully counteracting the work of the Church of England."[14] Keate maintained that it was incorrect to call most Seychellois Catholics; the mulattoes and released slaves, he said, were "heathens." He invited the Catholics to employ a priest for their own benefit at their own expense, but when a Catholic priest from Aden—Père Leon des Avanchers—applied for permission to reside at Mahé and act as priest in 1851, Keate denied permission and refused to allow des Avanchers to leave his ship. The matter was referred to London when des Avancher's ship was seen off by "practically the entire population." Two years later, London allowed two Catholic priests and the Sisters of Charity to establish permanent residence in the Seychelles; Catholicism has never looked back since.

Despite the loyalty of most Seychellois to Catholicism, there is a sense in which both Catholic and Protestant churches are, like government, alien institutions. Burton Benedict, who carried out extensive surveys in the Seychelles in 1960 and then updated them in 1970, has pointed out that all three have historically been run by foreigners whose outlook and morality have been quite different from that of the ordinary Seychellois. In Benedict's words:

> The Seychellois has had a long tradition of receiving orders from above. His fate has rested in the hands of slave-owners, employers, government officials. The Church fits closely into this pattern. Priests are approached for aid in obtaining jobs or welfare in much the same way employers or government officials are approached. The priest may be told lies for he is essentially part of an alien system. Many Seychellois are cynical about the Church which they claim is always trying to milk them for money. They point to the higher standard of living enjoyed by priests and to the amount of land the Church owns and the low rate of wages they pay.[15]

MAGIC AND WITCHCRAFT

Benedict and a number of other observers have argued that it is because of the lack of relevance of the church to the immediate lives of the Seychellois that they turn so frequently to sorcery, witchcraft, and magic. The church has strongly disapproved of such "superstitions" and has especially condemned the tendency of many Seychellois to use Christian saints as agents of vengeance in a complex web of beliefs associated with "malfaisance" (literally "evil-doing"). Benedict explained that "the fact that the Church strongly disapproves of these practices does not convince [the Seychellois] that they are wrong, but that they are in a different area not touched by the Church . . . the Church is for the people rather than of the people . . . many of the most serious problems about which Seychellois feel the greatest uncertainty are not dealt with by the Church and are believed to be outside its interests."[16]

For whatever reason, it is clear that people in the Seychelles see no contradiction between their beliefs in magic, witchcraft, sorcery, grisgris (evil charms), and malfaisance on the one hand and their standing as good Catholics or Protestants on the other. Benedict pointed out that witchcraft or sorcery provides a means for coping with imponderables that are beyond one's control. If a person loses his job, his status, his spouse, or his health, he tends to blame someone—an enemy or an ill-wisher—and he often identifies the person or force by consulting a local seer, sorcier, or sorcière. Seychellois seers are usually called *bon homme de bois* or *bonne femme de bois*; they are often older people who use simple fortune-telling devices like packs of cards, seeds, pebbles, tea or coffee strainings, mirrors, or palm-reading and relatively common divining techniques, often based on ambiguous statements and a deep knowledge of human foibles.

Associated with sorcery is the widespread use of amulets or talismans, which can afford protection or hold a man's attention, and evil charms (often called gris-gris) that can magically harm others in a spirit of vengeance. Gris-gris is a West African word that reached France from some of its possessions there and was brought to the Seychelles by the early settlers. It refers, when used properly, to a protective charm or a person who pretends to some supernatural powers by the possession of such a fetish. Benedict found that most gris-gris charms in the Seychelles are "small packets an inch or two square containing small bits of iron, a cooked potion, urine, semen, menstrual blood or hair of the intended victim," which are usually put in a private place like the bedclothes or washing utensils of an intended victim so that he or she may come into direct contact with them.[17] In recent times, however, the term "gris-gris" has come to be associated with almost any kind of soothsaying.

As far back as 1958 the government passed an ordinance outlawing witchcraft, fortune-telling, and the possession of items commonly used for sorcery, but Benedict still found such practices "very widespread" in 1970 and was under the impression that "restrictive legislation and clerical disapproval are less likely to be effective in stamping it out than improved social and economic conditions."[18] The persistence of gris-gris in the 1970s and 1980s is attested to by a series of raids on gris-gris houses carried out by the police, as a result of which several dozen people were arrested and large numbers of gris-gris materials confiscated.[19] According to Police Commissioner James Pillay, two of the major problems involved in enforcing the 1958 law are that (1) "a lot of people, including some in the [police] force . . . subscribe to the gris-gris service"; and (2) "people who practice gris-gris have a lot of money," which they presumably use to bribe or otherwise buy their way around the law. Because of the economic power of the practitioners and the widespread belief in magic, Pillay did not feel that gris-gris houses can be eliminated immediately, but he promised to "continue harassing that sort of people until the country is rid of it."

A somewhat more respectable form of "magic" that is widely practiced in the Seychelles is herbal doctoring, sometimes associated with gris-gris and sorcery because all three are often practiced by the same person. As witchcraft is against the law while herbal healing is not, gris-gris practitioners will often use their herbal medicine as a front for illegal magical practices. Such practices are usually tolerated by the police so long as they are "neither homicidal nor ostentatiously lucrative."[20] Wendy Veevers-Carter has explained the dynamics of the situation as follows:

> . . . their illegality lends the required titivation for the sophisticated and en-sures that the number of practitioners is limited to the cleverer or more dar-ing. In general, known "witches" are more respected than feared—by the whites, by the well-educated. But the lower classes are as enthralled by the possibility of bad magic being performed on them as by the fear of God himself, and perhaps more so.[21]

It should perhaps be pointed out that not all herbal practices in the Seychelles are fronts for *bons hommes de bois* or *bonnes femmes de bois.* There are a number of common herbal remedies that are known to have been at least somewhat efficacious over the years, and some herbalists have gained exceptional reputations. Perhaps the most successful of them all was a man named Charles Dialor (or Zialor) who died on Mahé at the age of 91 in 1962. Dialor was so successful in treating patients who had been abandoned by allopathic doctors that many Western doctors in the Seychelles were known to have advised patients whose ailments they could not cure to "try Dialor."[22]

LANGUAGE AND EDUCATION

The argument that both Catholicism and Anglicanism are divorced from the lives of most Seychellois is paralleled by the argument that the French and English languages have also failed to have any meaningful impact on the vast majority of the people. French has always had great snob appeal in the Seychelles as the language of the original white set-tlers and the major attribute setting them off from the English and Africans. The French were not anxious to teach their language to the others—they never established schools, for example, during the fifty-eight years that they ruled the colony—and, like the French everywhere, they had great disdain for the non-French, English and Creole alike. Veevers-Carter depicted the Seychellois French *grands blancs* (the descendants of the original French settlers) as being people "vain about their use of the French language, [who] regard their homes as last bas-tions in the lapping sea of creole and English all around them."[23]

But Veevers-Carter also pointed out that their pride in French is "the Frenchest thing" about the *grands blancs.* They have always viewed themselves as cultivated and worldly aristocrats, but they have gained a reputation among the British and Creole populations as having an inflated notion of themselves. Few of them speak French without Creole words and usages, fewer still can afford the kind of easy luxury they aspire to. Most of them have survived as planters by paying their laborers very little, keeping the black population "down," and working fairly hard themselves. Their Catholicism, like that of the black Seychellois, is "deplorably superstitious [and] rather lax in all but the ostentatious aspects of the Catholic religion"; their French meals, although elaborate, "retain nothing of French éclat or delicacy."[24]

Some idea of the size of the population that considers itself French *grand blanc* can be gained from language statistics collected in 1971, in which it was determined that 1.9 percent of the population uses French as the principal language of the home.[25] French has been required as a second language in the schools from the fourth year of studies onwards, but the 1971 survey indicated that only 29.4 percent of the Seychellois were able to speak French. Many older people in the Seychelles still use French in formal situations and in correspondence, reflecting the prestige of the language. French is also the main language used by the Catholic church, although the role of Creole is increasing.

Creole has always been and still is the language used most frequently outside the classroom and in private conversations. It is usually described as a French-based patois similar to that found in Mauritius, Haiti, or Louisiana, but many linguists are beginning to describe it as a distinctive language in its own right. Perhaps the most that can be said at this point is that Seychelles Creole is essentially an eighteenth-century French that has developed in relative isolation and has borrowed words from Malagasy, Bantu languages, Hindi, and English. Its syntax is Bantu and French, and it is widely infused with words and dialects of southwest France, brought to the Seychelles by French sailors.[26] Some linguists argue that it is not a distinct language because it has no orthography and cannot express abstractions, but it impresses even the unknowing as an especially effective means of expression for storytelling and singing as well as everyday conversation.

The British introduced English into the syllabus in the schools in 1880, at which point English and French became the only two "official" languages in the Colony. Teaching, however, remained in the vernacular until 1944, when English was made the compulsory medium of instruction and French was retained as a second language required of all students from the fourth year of schooling. Even as late as 1966 however, Webb reported that Creole was still the most effective means of communication in the schools. "If you seek an answer in English or French [in the schools today]," Webb wrote in 1966, "you must first explain the question in Creole."[27]

A frequent criticism of the British is that they did a great disservice to the Seychelles by casually ruling them for 162 years, all the while allowing Catholicism, the French language, and the Napoleonic Civil Code to become bastardized by the Creole population. Because of Britain's relative lack of interest in the colony, the Seychelles are probably the most extreme example one can find of a laissez-faire colonial situation, in which the Seychellois were quite free to develop (or fail to develop) on their own. The British government in the Seychelles ran no schools or welfare programs until 1947, when Dr. Percy Selwyn-Clarke was made governor. Prior to that time, the government simply provided an inspectorate and modest grants-in-aid to church school missions. Selwyn-Clarke took over some schools and started others, initiated a medical health service, reorganized the hospital in Victoria and the leper colony on Curieuse Island, built new houses, undertook new town planning and building programs, and instituted a number of social reforms. Within a few years, however, the wealthy sectors of the Seychellois population objected to Selwyn-Clarke's "socialism," and he was succeeded, beginning in 1952, by a string of much more easy-going and less ambitious administrators.[28]

The role of English in the Seychelles has increased steadily since the decision to make it the compulsory language of instruction. In 1971 English was the language in the home for only 3 percent of the population, but 37.7 percent of the Seychellois were able to use English as a second or third language and approximately 82 percent of those under 15 years of age were able to read English. Curiously enough, English was also listed by a large number of Seychellois in 1971 as the preferred language for intimate conversations and lovemaking.[29]

English is today the official language of the National Assembly, but a member may address the Assembly in Creole or French as well. Creole is spoken by 95 percent of the people and is read by more than 50 percent. There is very little Creole literature in existence, as there is no official Creole orthography, but it is possible to write and read Creole texts by using conventional French or English orthography with phonetic modifications. Creole is now used regularly in radio broadcasts (for an estimated 25–30 percent of total broadcasting time), in most public (and especially political) speeches, in some churches, and in several newspapers. (*Echo des Isles*, a Catholic mission paper, sometimes has dialogues or interviews in Creole; *Vie et Action*, a Catholic youth monthly, is entirely in Creole; and the official government newspaper, *Nation*, often runs articles in Creole.) The Anglican church has under way a major project designed to translate the Bible into Seychellois

Creole, and the government is preparing a scheme to introduce Creole as a medium of instruction in the schools.

CLASS, STATUS, AND RACE

Although race is extremely important in determining individual status in Seychelles, social classes cannot be delineated strictly on the basis of skin color. Unlike Mauritius, where Indian, Chinese, and French communities have tended to remain quite separate from one another, Seychelles has witnessed interbreeding between communities to a degree unknown almost anywhere else in the world. Since much of this interbreeding has been done outside the institution of marriage, it is extremely difficult to know the exact racial background of almost anyone in the society. It is common to find within the same family or domestic group, for example, children who exhibit a variety of different racial backgrounds, ranging from those with the blackest Negroid features through the mulattoes and those with Sinic or Indian characteristics to the most European-looking *grands blancs*. James Mancham, the first president of the Seychelles, was born of French-Chinese ancestry on his father's side and French-Creole ancestry on his mother's side, but his son is by a British ex-wife. President France Albert René, who is as European in appearance as anyone on any of the islands, is widely believed to be the illegitimate son of a French sea captain and a Creole mother; René's stepson Francis, son of his second wife, has handsome, almost classic, mulatto features.

There are some extremely poor whites and very wealthy blacks in the Seychelles, but high status is, nonetheless, generally attached to light skin and pedigrees from Europe. Benedict found a universal claim to European ancestry, even among those Seychellois with the blackest skin and most Negroid attributes.[30] He also found that Seychellois commonly refer to themselves as *blanc*, *rouge*, or *noir*, usually with descending degrees of pride. One of the reasons for so many interracial marriages and sexual alliances in the Seychelles is clearly the attempt on the part of many Seychellois (and especially women) to produce offspring who are light in skin color.

In this milieu, one can identify two broad historical social classes, distinguished essentially by property, income, and occupation but frequently reinforced by skin color and cultural behavior. In the upper class are the French *grands blancs*, who have historically controlled the landed estates and plantations, plus a small number of Britons and expatriates (mostly consultants and investors) engaged primarily in business, commerce, and government. Slightly less prestigeful but still predominantly upper-class is the very small segment of Indians and

Chinese, with the Indians historically tending to dominate the wholesale and import-export trade and the Chinese being prominent in retailing (there are small segments of both the Indian and Chinese communities that are without property or wealth and are distinctly lower-class). Until 1931 the Indians and Chinese were classified separately in the census, but racial classifications were abolished in 1935 and everyone has since been described in the census as Seychellois. The lower class is historically a laboring class that has owned little property and has struggled for dignified employment. In recent years a middle-ranking class of civil servants, white-collar workers, small proprietors, and skilled workers has been emerging.

Some idea of the size of these various classes can be gained by looking at income figures, such as those in Table 2.1. These figures were compiled by the census organization from a random sample of 483 households (4 percent of the total) in 1978. Although there was a uniform tendency for respondents in the study to understate their incomes, the results obtained indicate a clear division of Seychellois society into three distinct income groups. The elite upper group, consisting of less than 3 percent of the population, has a reported average gross monthly income of Rs. (rupees) 6,670 (US $1,112; $US1 = Rs.6.25). The much larger middle class, which accounts for about a quarter of the population in the sample, has an average monthly income of Rs.2,801 (US $467). In sharp contrast, the sizable lower class (71.5 percent of the total) grosses on an average only Rs.858 (US$143) per month. The minimum monthly expenditures considered necessary for a family of four to exist without malnutrition is estimated by the Ministry of Labour Health and Welfare at Rs.1,166 in 1978.[31] As can be seen from Table 2.1, both the middle and upper classes have monthly incomes well above this minimum while the average monthly income of the lower classes (at least as reported to the government) is well below it.

Perhaps because the economic gap between classes is so great, Seychellois, and especially women, are extremely status-conscious, with much of their time spent trying to improve their social position. When one is seeking to move up in status individually (as opposed to class or group mobility) a light skin often provides a social and economic advantage, in ways that have been detailed by Benedict:

> A light-skinned person is more apt to be engaged in a managerial capacity than a dark-skinned person. A light-skinned person has opportunities for emigration (e.g. to Australia). . . . Those with light skins will not marry those with dark though they will have sexual relations and may even set up a ménage. Exceptions which prove the rule are cases of dark-skinned but prosperous or successful men marrying light-skinned girls. The girl and her family overlook the man's dark pigmentation in favour of his economic

TABLE 2.1

Monthly Income Distribution by Households, 1978

	Average Gross Income	Number of Households	Percentage of Total Households
Upper class	Rs. 6,670	14	2.9
Middle class	Rs. 2,801	124	25.6
Lower class	Rs. 858	345	71.5
Total	Rs.10,329	483	100.0

Source: Report on the 1978 Household Expenditure Survey (Victoria: Government Printing Office, September 1979), pp. 67ff.

and social standing. At the lowest economic level those with light skins cite their colour as evidence of their social superiority. This claim is recognized by the darker skinned. In one settlement there was a white man who was notorious as a drunkard, scoundrel and wifebeater, yet he was always able to get a woman to live with him because he was white. Neighbours, both light and dark, admitted this.[32]

Given the importance of race in determining social status, it is surprising that Seychelles has been something of a haven from racial tension, with very little cultural or physical distance publicly separating any of the races and few racial incidents of any kind. For more than a century blacks, whites, Indians, and Chinese have gone to the same schools, where whites have typically received fewer prizes than Indians, Chinese or, lately, blacks. In any business, school, shop, or social gathering—whether on the beach or indoors—people from all races now mix freely and have done so historically, without any visible cultural barrier. Veevers-Carter concluded that "racial and linguistic groups do mix more freely here than any other place I have been to, and minorities who withhold their approval are forced—no matter what their private thoughts—to acquiesce."[33]

DOMESTIC GROUPS

Although hypocrisy about race is present in the Seychelles, the islands are distinguished from most other places in the world by their remarkably liberal patterns of courtship and marriage. Interracial marriages, pregnancies before marriage, and sexual relationships outside wedlock all seem to be the rule rather than the exception. Some studies have estimated that three of five Seychellois women are pregnant when they marry, and many tales of sailors and tourists revolve around the sexual promiscuity of both women and men. Benedict found that only 18 percent of his urban sample and 29 percent of his rural sample lived in nuclear families as defined in Europe and America, and a 1979 study found that only 58 percent of all Seychellois children live in family unions with both of their natural parents.[34] Most adults in the Seychelles live in de facto unions known locally as "en ménage," which led Benedict to call Seychellois households "domestic groups" rather than families.

Benedict's studies show conclusively that the tendency to live en ménage has been increasing in the Seychelles throughout the twentieth century, and recent figures confirm this trend into the 1980s. The marriage rate was about 9.5 per 1,000 in 1891–1893, but it declined to 7.4 per 1,000 in 1897, to 6.2 per 1,000 in 1959, to 5.4 per 1,000 in 1968, and to 4.7 per 1,000 in 1980.[35] Only 59.2 percent of Seychellois women have ever been married at the end of their reproductive period (age 45–49), compared with 85–90 percent in France and the United Kingdom and nearly 98 percent in most Asian countries. In the 1890s an average of 26.8 percent of children born in the Seychelles were acknowledged as illegitimate; by the 1960s the average had risen to 44.3 percent. In 1980, almost two-thirds (64 percent) of all children born in the Seychelles were born out of wedlock (see Table 2.2).

Why do so many men and women choose to live en ménage in the Seychelles? De facto unions are disapproved of by both church and state, and people themselves willingly agree that marriage is preferable to a de facto union. And yet the practice is widespread and is rapidly increasing.

Benedict explained the practice in terms of the "expenses and difficulties surrounding legal marriage" and the prevalence of certain cultural ideas concerning dependency relationships within the "domestic group." To begin with, divorce is not sanctioned by the Roman Catholic church and civil divorces are difficult and expensive to obtain (in the late 1970s fewer than a dozen divorces were granted in any given year in the whole of Seychelles). Under these circumstances, living en ménage becomes a solution, not only for people who have tried and failed at marriage but also for young people who are not certain that they want to marry the person with whom they are living. Table 2.3 indicates that the number of illegitimate children (a sure sign of ménage arrangements) is far greater for women in their teenage years than it is for those in their 20s and 30s, but the tendency remains strong right up to the age of 40. Benedict has made it clear that widows and widowers are among those who frequently set up en ménage, as do middle-aged people from broken (or breaking) marriages.

TABLE 2.2

Legitimate and Illegitimate Children Born
in Seychelles, 1971-1980

Year	Legitimate Children Born	Illegitimate Children Born	Total Born	Percentage Illegitimate
1971	1,015	822	1,837	45
1972	885	831	1,716	48
1973	854	785	1,639	48
1974	896	964	1,860	52
1975	842	964	1,806	53
1976	730	912	1,642	56
1977	626	974	1,599	61
1978	713	1,083	1,796	60
1979	637	1,093	1,730	63
1980	661	1,169	1,830	64

Source: Republic of Seychelles, Statistical Abstract, 1979
(Victoria: Government Printers, August 1980), p. 89; and
Republic of Seychelles, Statistical Bulletin, Fourth Quarter,
1980, Vol. 1, no. 3 (Victoria: Government Printers, February
1981), p. 4.

TABLE 2.3

Legitimacy Status and Age of Mother, 1979

Age of Mother	Total Births	Legitimate	Illegitimate	Percentage Illegitimate
Under 15	6	--	6	100
15-19	451	60	391	87
20-24	581	188	393	68
25-29	297	158	139	47
30-34	211	123	88	42
35-39	129	78	51	40
40+	55	51	4	7
Total	1,730	658	1,072	

Source: Republic of Seychelles, Statistical Abstract, 1979
(Victoria: Government Printers, August 1980), p. 9.

But explanations of the custom of living en ménage must go far beyond those given above. Benedict found a tradition of living in de facto unions that prevailed for generations in some families, and he also found that among those living en ménage in urban areas, a surprising 40.5 percent were in unions in which the woman was older than the man.[36] He explained this latter phenomenon by pointing to a coincidence in the towns of large numbers of widows and other women whose previous unions have broken down and a steady influx into the towns of unattached young men looking for work. Benedict also speculated that the mother-son tie, which is very close in the Seychelles, "finds its analogue in the ménage of a young man with an older woman," but he was quick to point out that such an hypothesis "clearly requires further testing by intensive psychological methods."[37]

One of the ways to understand the tendency for Seychellois to live in de facto unions is to focus on the gap between the ideals and realities of society. In the upper-income groups, among the *grands blancs*, women are invariably married to the men with whom they are living. Their social position is dependent on their maintaining a "respectable" pattern of behavior, which is defined in large part by sexual fidelity to their husbands. A woman of high status in the Seychelles is not to be seen habitually in the presence of a man other than her husband, although she is expected to turn a blind eye to her husband's extramarital relationships with lower-class women. This is "a pattern which dates from the earliest settlement of the Seychelles when Europeans set the pattern by their willingness to have sexual relations with black or coloured women. The heterogeneity of the population as to pigmentation and other physical characteristics testifies to the prevalence of this form of mating."[38]

Poor people in the Seychelles also consider Christian marriage as the ideal form of union, and they try to emulate upper-income groups by carefully arranging marriages and making suitable alliances with leading families. For the poor, however, marriage opportunities and possibilities are much more restricted than for the wealthy, especially if one is dark-skinned. Benedict found, for example, that a female schoolteacher with dark skin will often find it quite difficult to marry. On the basis of her occupation she is expected to marry someone who is fairly high-ranking, but her dark pigmentation is associated with low status. On the other hand, a very poor girl with a light skin and a good reputation may be able to marry a successful man with a dark skin and move up in status, even though her family will often disapprove.

A major set of factors encouraging the establishment of de facto unions has to do with the extremely high costs of weddings and the establishment of households. Benedict estimated that even a poor wedding costs a year's wages for the average laborer, as every wedding is ac-

companied by an elaborate reception with an all-night drinking and
dancing party held after the ceremony.[39] The families of both the bride
and groom contribute to the cost of the reception about equally, a practice that provides fertile ground for disputes and bad feelings of all kinds.
What all this means is that

> . . . both sides must approve of the union and keep approving of it during
> the long months of preparation. In addition to the costs of the reception
> there is the bride's trousseau and the furniture for the house and perhaps
> the house itself – all of which must be made. Sometimes it is several years
> before all these arrangements have been carried out. The longer the period
> the greater the danger that a ménage will be set up by one or the other and
> that negotiations will fall through, or that, when the marriage finally occurs
> the couple will split up very soon afterwards, a not infrequent occur-
> rence.[40]

The increasing tendency for people to live en ménage can be explained by the heightened economic pressures of the 1970s and 1980s, a
worldwide tendency toward more liberal social values (which is visible
to the Seychellois because of their increased contacts outside), and the
cultural accumulations associated with the custom in the Seychelles
itself. A young woman growing up in the Seychelles today is under enormous pressure to set up her own household and have her own children,
in part because these give her status and influence in society, in part
because they free her from dependence on her mother. So long as a
young woman is with her mother, she is under "constant surveillance"
because "the mother wants to guard her reputation in the hope of making
a good marriage for her."[41] Seychellois teenagers have also been prone to
revolt because the age of consent was historically 21 and is still 18, both
relatively high figures compared to other Asian and African countries.[42]
    With women all around her living en ménage, and with marriage
arrangements terribly expensive and interminably delayed, a young
woman will often decide to persuade a man to take her out of her parents
home as a wife or ménagère. The obvious way to do this is to become
pregnant, which accounts for a good deal of the seeming promiscuity in
Seychellois society and for the exceptionally large number of illegitimate
children born to teenage women. It also accounts for the fact that more
than one out of every four children born in the Seychelles in the 1970s
and 1980s has been born to a teenage mother, the largest such percentage
in any country in the world.[43] From the male perspective, a young man is
encouraged to leave his mother's house not only because of the sexual opportunity but also to gain greater freedom and more control over his own
earnings, and because a teenage son will frequently have strained relations with his mother's husband or ménager. Attempts by the government

to divert teenagers from the custom of living en ménage will be discussed in Chapter 4.

Seychellois women and men are often thought by outsiders to be especially promiscuous and erotic, a view encouraged by customs that produce a good deal of flirtatiousness on the part of both sexes from an early age. Alec Waugh, for example, described Seychellois women as "tender, caressing, ardent, gracious, natural and utterly unvicious." A U.S. journalist has said that "they're French enough to have good shapes, English enough to have good manners, Asian enough to have a touch of the exotic about them, and African enough to have the call of the wild in them."[44] Ozanne has called the Seychelles woman "the acme of eroticism" and has explained her behavior as follows:

> It is not that the Seychelles girl is immoral. She is not, but she is absolutely and completely amoral. In other words, morals, to her mind, do not enter into matters relating to sex. It does not occur to her that she is sinning in obeying a sex impulse; to her way of thinking, it is no more immoral . . . than . . . for her to eat a bowl of rice because she felt hungry. . . . Neither does it occur to those who accept payment that they are doing anything out of the ordinary. If a man is such a fool as to give them money for doing what they would be quite willing to do free, this is his lookout.[45]

In fact, however, there are very few professional prostitutes in the Seychelles, and liaisons between men and women do take place according to a fairly structured set of rules. A woman will usually live with one man at a time, for extended periods, and will try to bear children by him. Only a very promiscuous woman will not know the fathers of her children, and she will invariably claim to know them. Benedict found that the ménage arrangements he studied lasted for an average of about seven years, as compared with seventeen to eighteen years for Seychellois marriages, there being a number of less stable forms of union (affairs without residence, intermittent relationships, or casual sexual encounters with *"une passant"* – a passer-by).[46] As with upper-class Seychellois, it is expected that women in the middle and lower classes will remain faithful to the men they are living with, even though there is no such expectation for men.

In contrast to the view of outsiders, most Seychellois women view their sexual activities from the perspective of their responsibilities to their children and perhaps to a few other close kin. Nevertheless, there is no appreciation of the extended family stretching back through the generations, as there is, for example, in India. Indeed, genealogical knowledge usually does not extend back for more than three generations, and one's commitment to "family" is not nearly as intense as it is in India, or even historically in the West. Unlike the situation in India,

Seychellois women are remarkably well educated, and they generally work outside the home. The 1977 census reported, for example, that there were more females than males in Seychellois schools and almost three out of five (59.9 percent) of women aged 15–55 were employed.[47] Most Seychellois women try to keep their children living with them, the children usually adopting the woman's name when a ménage breaks up. The 1979 study found that only 14 percent of Seychellois children were living without their mothers, but 39 percent were living without their fathers.[48] Women unquestionably tend to be the dominant partners in families and domestic groups.

In this atmosphere, Benedict explained, a woman "will treat her husband well, but if the household is a poor one and her husband neglects her she must be on the lookout for ways to help herself and her children. One of these ways is by granting sexual favours in the hopes of aid."[49] Benedict found that a number of women in his surveys felt that they could not afford to refuse the proprietors of the estates on which they worked or the masters of the houses in which they were domestics, because that person might be helpful to them or to any resultant children. Many women also argued that it was better to have an affair with a married man than a single man, as married men were more likely to help a mistress in order to keep her from creating difficulties with a wife. The illegitimate child of a wealthy father can usually expect to receive employment, gifts, or other favors from him. If a man is truly pleased with his *ménagère* or his offspring, he may allow the latter to use his name rather than the name of the mother. In all these instances, such dispensations by the father redound to the credit and comfort of the mother, there being much less stigma attached to illegitimacy in the Seychelles than almost anywhere else in the world.

Perhaps the most remarkable thing about Seychellois society is the way in which people are very proper about things that they consider to be consistent with Western concepts of human dignity, in an environment where many of their values are quite different from those of the West. There is virtually no bargaining or haggling about prices in the marketplace, for example, even though prices are universally considered to be high, most people are struggling to make a living, and products are not nearly as standardized as in Europe or America. To haggle about a price, much less to beg, is considered beneath the dignity of even the poor Seychellois. Women will make enormous sacrifices in terms of food and other necessities for their children in order to clothe them well, or to have at least one piece of stunning furniture in the home, or to have a fine dress and hat for Mass on Sundays, even though none of these externalities fool anyone into thinking that the woman is all that well-off. The corollary of the frequently heard proposition that a "good" woman in the

Seychelles is someone who can look after herself and her children is the statement by one of Benedict's informants, that a "bad woman" was someone who cohabited with men who she knew would not help her.[50]

QUESTIONS ABOUT SOCIAL CHANGE

It is possible to view Seychellois society from a romantic perspective, and even to wish that somehow its liberality, particularly as regards racial and sexual interaction, could continue to survive and flourish in the modern age. But the suffering associated with teenage pregnancies and widespread illegitimacy of children has led most observers, and most Seychelles leaders, to consideration of far-reaching societal reforms. As has already been indicated, people in the Seychelles live en ménage and have illegitimate children, often as teenagers, not because they consider such practices the most desirable, but rather because they feel economic and social pressures resulting from the widespread poverty that exists on the islands. The incidence of drug consumption among younger men and liquor consumption among both men and women has increased at frightening rates since the mid-1960s, to the point where the Seychelles now rank third or fourth in the world in per capita liquor consumption.[51] Syphilis, gonorrhea, and other venereal diseases are, as one might expect, rampant.

More than any government before it, the present government is determined to bring about sweeping changes in society, particularly among youth. Having come to power by a coup d'etat, it views itself as revolutionary and socialist. In its first four years in power, it demonstrated its willingness to use the coercive power of the state to take over schools, medical facilities, private property, and businesses, and to force children into a variety of socializing institutions, all ostensibly for the purpose of bettering the lot of the common people. The economic and social changes sweeping the islands are analyzed and assessed in Chapters 4 and 5, but before proceeding to those topics it is necessary to provide some understanding of the political system, which has become the great driving force of change in the last quarter of the twentieth century.

NOTES

1. The population was 61,898 according to the 1977 census. Projections for 1981 appear in Republic of Seychelles, *Statistical Bulletin, Third Quarter, 1980*, Vol. 1, no. 2 (November 1980), p. 10.
2. Republic of Seychelles, *Statistical Bulletin, Fourth Quarter, 1980*, Vol. 1, no. 3 (February 1981), p. 2.
3. Figures are from the *1977 Census Report* (Victoria: Government Printers,

April 1978), pp. 45ff.

4. Republic of Seychelles, *Statistical Abstract, 1979* (Victoria: Government Printer, August 1980), p. 16.

5. Based on interviews with members of the Planning Ministry, Victoria, June 1981.

6. Maxime Fayon, *Geography of Seychelles,* 2nd rev. ed. (Victoria: Ministry of Education and Culture, 1978), pp. 21–22.

7. *Statistical Abstract, 1979,* p. 8, and *Statistical Bulletin, Fourth Quarter, 1980,* pp. 2, 12.

8. *Statistical Abstract, 1979,* p. 17.

9. *Recherche et Réflexion sur la société Seychelloise: Une Définition des Problèmes sociaux* [Research and reflection on Seychellois society: A definition of social problems] (Victoria: Social Service Division, Ministry of Works and Social Service, 1980), p. 78.

10. A thorough recent study of employment in Seychelles is *Employment and Poverty in the Seychelles: Report of a Study Organised by the Institute of Development Studies* (Brighton: University of Sussex, 1980). This study was conducted for the government of Seychelles and was chaired by Percy Selwyn.

11. A.W.T. Webb, *The Story of Seychelles,* 3rd rev. ed. (Victoria: Government Printing Office, 1966), p. 37.

12. Quoted from interviews with Anglican church leaders in Seychelles.

13. Burton Benedict, *People of the Seychelles,* 3rd ed., Ministry of Overseas Development, Overseas Research Publication No. 14 (London: Her Majesty's Stationery Office, 1970), p. 14.

14. *Story of Seychelles,* p. 38.

15. Benedict, *People of the Seychelles,* p. 64. In a new book on the Seychelles, Marion Benedict has detailed how a Seychelloise was on the way to becoming a witch over a fifteen-year period. See Burton Benedict and Marion Benedict, *Men, Women and Money in Seychelles: Two Views* (Berkeley: University of California Press, forthcoming 1982).

16. Benedict, *People of the Seychelles,* pp. 64–65.

17. Ibid., p. 62.

18. Ibid., p. 64.

19. An interview with Commissioner Pillay appears in "Police Hit at Gris-Gris," *Weekend Life* (Victoria weekly), Vol. 1, no. 32 (February 4, 1978), p. 1. All quotations in this paragraph are from this interview.

20. Quoted from an interview with a Seychelles police official, November 1979.

21. Wendy Day Veevers-Carter, *Island Home* (New York: Random House, 1970), p. 338.

22. Quoted from Guy Lionnet, *The Seychelles,* (Harrisburg, Pa.: Stackpole Books, 1972), p. 112.

23. Veevers-Carter, *Island Home,* p. 331.

24. Ibid., p. 330.

25. For a summary of official language statistics for Seychelles, from which the statistics included here are drawn, see Chris Corne, *Seychelles Creole Grammar: Elements for Indian Ocean Proto-Creole Reconstruction* (Tubingen: TBL Verlag

Gunter Narr, 1977), pp. 3ff.

26. An excellent discussion of language and other cultural factors appears in Lionnet, *Seychelles*, pp. 111ff.

27. Webb, *Story of Seychelles*, p. 43.

28. F. D. Ommanney, *The Shoals of Capricorn* (London: Longmans Green and Company, 1952), p. 190. A detailed personal assessment of Selwyn-Clarke's years as governor appears in Alec Waugh, *Where the Clocks Chime Twice* (London: Cassell and Company, 1952), pp. 153–163, 198–208.

29. Corne, *Seychelles Creole Grammar*, p. 3.

30. Benedict, *People of the Seychelles*, p. 55.

31. Republic of Seychelles, Ministry of Labour Health and Welfare, *Report of National Conference on Employment, Manpower, Incomes and Production* (Victoria: Government Printing Office, September 1978), p. 45.

32. Benedict, *People of the Seychelles*, p. 55.

33. Veevers-Carter, *Island Home*, pp. 335–336.

34. See Benedict, *People of the Seychelles*, p. 29, and *Nou Bane Zanfans: A Report and Working Paper for the Seychelles International Year of the Child Commission*, a large-scale study prepared by Pamela Richardson and Jon Wegge (Victoria: Government Printers, September 15, 1979), p. 5.

35. Figures prior to 1980 in this and the following paragraphs, unless otherwise noted, are from Benedict, *People of the Seychelles*. Figures for 1980 and 1981 are from interviews with census officials in Victoria except where footnoted otherwise.

36. Benedict, *People of the Seychelles*, p. 48. Benedict's work is still the classic study of Seychelles society; there is nothing approaching it for thoroughness and sensitivity. As indicated in the footnotes, the following section is heavily dependent on Benedict's analysis, although attempts have been made to update it whenever possible.

37. Ibid., p. 45.

38. Ibid., p. 46.

39. Ibid., pp. 46–47.

40. Ibid., p. 47.

41. Ibid.

42. The thought was elaborated during interviews with family planning and welfare workers in Seychelles in 1978 and 1981.

43. *Nation* (Victoria daily), Vol. 5, no. 6 (January 10, 1981), p. 1.

44. The quotes are from Douglas Alexander, *Holiday in Seychelles: A Guide to the Islands* (Capetown: Purnell Publishers, 1972), p. 39.

45. J.A.F. Ozanne, *Coconuts and Creoles* (London: Philip Allan and Company, 1936), pp. 140–141.

46. Benedict, *People of the Seychelles*, p. 45.

47. *1977 Census Report*, pp. 68, 81–83.

48. *Nou Bane Zanfans*, p. 5.

49. Benedict, *People of the Seychelles*, p. 48.

50. Ibid., p. 49.

51. Ralph Adam, "La jeunesse dans une société en changement" [Youth in a changing society] in *Recherche et réflexion*, p. 40.

3

Politics

In the early morning of 5 June 1977 sixty Seychellois men in camouflage uniforms, armed with Soviet and East European–made rifles, were tendered onto the island of Mahé, off the *Mapinduzi* (Swahili for "revolution"), a Tanzanian ship commissioned to ferry guerrillas around the Indian Ocean. Together with 120 more men, armed with sticks from the forest and a few walkie-talkies, the 60 Tanzanian-trained guerrillas captured two police stations, the armory, the radio station, and the president's office, thereby overthrowing the democratically elected government of James R. Mancham, the first president of Seychelles, who had assumed office when the country became independent from Britain on 29 June 1976.[1] The new government, which is headed by Mancham's prime minister, France Albert René, has styled itself a revolutionary socialist government and has established a one-party system. For most Seychellois, the coup was final proof that their country had at last crashed its way into the twentieth century.

MANCHAM AND THE FIRST GOVERNMENT

The "coup of sixty rifles" was engineered by René, in collaboration with Julius Nyerere, president of Tanzania. Both René and Nyerere had been appalled at the lifestyle of Mancham, who had gained an international reputation as a playboy. They also resented his close ties to Western capitalist interests and the freewheeling free-enterprise economy he had instituted in the Seychelles. Only 38 years old when he became president, Mancham could usually be seen with beautiful women and Arab millionaires at the beach hotels, having based his regime almost exclusively on his ability to attract Western capital for the development of tourism. During most of his tenure as president, Mancham was out jet-setting in Europe, America, the Persian Gulf, or the Far East, looking for potential investors for a number of projects that he and his government had designed. When the coup took place, Mancham was

49

Figure 3.1. Jacques Hodoul (white shirt), presently Minister of Foreign Affairs, and James Michel (rifle on back), Minister of Information, being congratulated by Tanzanian advisers after the coup d'etat of 5 June 1977. Some of the Seychellois that carried rifles during the coup are also pictured in their battle fatigues. These men have since formed the core of the new Seychelles Liberation Army.

staying in a US $300-a-day suite at the Savoy Hotel in London, where he had gone to attend a Commonwealth conference.

Mancham was so tied to the Western capitalist world that he and his Seychelles Democratic party (SDP) had even advocated until 1974 that the Seychelles remain a part of Great Britain rather than seek independent nationhood. If the United States could have its Hawaii and France its Tahiti, Mancham used to argue, why couldn't Britain have its Seychelles? The answer was provided by René, who formed a rival political party, the Seychelles People's United party (SPUP) and began to attract voters on a platform of complete independence, forcing Mancham to come out for separate nationhood. The SDP managed to beat the SPUP in the April 1974 elections, garnering thirteen of fifteen seats in the national assembly, but because his party had secured only 52.4 percent of the vote Mancham decided to bring René's SPUP (with 47.6 percent) into a coalition government.[2] René and his colleagues later argued that a coup was necessary because Mancham was planning to abrogate the con-

Figure 3.2. President Julius Nyerere of Tanzania greeting Seychelles soldiers in Victoria after the 1977 coup. Training by the Tanzanian army and participation of Tanzanians in the coup were crucial to its success. Seychelles Agence Press.

stitution, install a one-party system, and suppress the opposition. Now René has done all three of these things himself.

Whatever his failings, Mancham clearly had the ability (and the propensity) to think big. Trained as a lawyer in London in the late 1950s and early 1960s, Mancham returned to the Seychelles to found a newspaper (the *Seychelles Weekly*) and a political party (the SDP) in 1963. He was elected to the legislature in 1964, at the age of 25. Six years later he was sworn in as the first Seychellois chief minister under the British.[3] Mancham's father, the wealthiest grocer in the Seychelles, and Mancham's wife, a striking blonde cosmetics saleswoman from Britain, tried to convince him that he should give up politics and other women, but Mancham eventually disappointed both of them. His father died of a heart attack in 1965 at the age of 54; his wife divorced him in 1975 after twelve years of marriage.

During the negotiations for the siting of the U.S. tracking station, Mancham was retained by the United States as an attorney with a watching brief.[4] In the late 1960s he was instrumental in mobilizing political support for construction of the airport. A one-man public relations

Figure 3.3. James R. Mancham, first President of the Seychelles, who was over-thrown in the coup d'etat of June 5, 1977. Mancham is pictured here with his New York girlfriend, jewelry designer Helga von Meyerhoffer Wagner, at the Taj Mahal in India in 1976. While visiting India as President, Mancham called Wagner his "first lady." Photo courtesy Press Trust of India.

department, Mancham traveled incessantly in the 1970s, using his flamboyant lifestyle and considerable persuasive powers to bring potential investors to the islands. Before the coup took place Mancham had toyed with the idea of making the Seychelles a tax haven for offshore banking and offshore insurance, offering it (like Liberia or Panama) as a flag of convenience for shipping, or developing it as a major mid-ocean drop-off and pick-up point for giant interocean container vessels that have found it uneconomic to distribute and collect small packets of goods in dozens of minor ports on the Indian Ocean littoral.

Mancham had also interested a consortium of big oil companies in offshore oil exploration, was in the process of developing secret hideaway spots for some of the wealthiest Arabs in the Gulf, and had launched a number of programs to lure rich tourists (like the employees of the oil companies in the Gulf) to the Seychelles. One of the most dramatic deals Mancham made was with Prince Sharam, son of the shah of Iran's sister, who was allowed to purchase the island of Darros for US $1 million and to hire a South African firm to install a private airstrip, complete with radio transmitters and radar. A second was with Saudi Arabian businessman Adnan Khashoggi—mentioned prominently in the Lockheed bribery scandal in the United States—who was allowed to buy 40 acres (16 hectares) of land near the Beau Vallon Hotel, on the main island of Mahé, for US $2.5 million.

Mancham's opponents argued that he was developing tourism at the expense of all else and that his lifestyle was an increasing embarrassment to the nation. Particularly unpopular was Mancham's information minister, David Joubert, who was often left in charge of the government when Mancham was out with the jet set. Joubert built a reputation for running up bills that he never paid, for carousing with women, and for being obnoxious when drunk. As one of Mancham's supporters put it after the coup, "Joubert was a good man when he was sober, but he rose too fast and got drunk too often; he, more than anyone else, ruined poor Mancham."[5]

THE RENÉ GOVERNMENT

Since the coup, the new government has made it clear that it is not opposed to tourism, but it has promised to develop the fishing industry and agriculture as relatively equal parts of a three-legged economic strategy for the future. The new government has also introduced a heavy surfeit of socialist and Marxist jargon into the press, which it now monopolizes, and has, accordingly, promised to equalize incomes. The Seychelles People's Progressive Front (SPPF), the new name of SPUP after René's attempt to combine all political parties in his one-party system, has openly set itself against a free press. Its policy statements argue that

> ... in a developing country, such as ours, there is no room for the so-called independent press of the capitalist countries. Every journalist must be committed to the cause of the people and the socialist construction of the country. If the press fails to contribute to this cause, it becomes an enemy of the people. The concept of the independent paper is misleading for it inevitably backs a certain group or groups, be it big business, a foreign power, or an ethnic group.[6]

The unquestioned leader of the new government is René, who, like Mancham, is a London-trained lawyer. Born on 16 November 1935, René comes from somewhat humbler origins than Mancham, having been raised as the son of a plantation manager on the island of Farquhar. René was a bright student who won scholarships at St. Joseph's Convent School, St. Louis Primary School, and at Seychelles College Secondary

School, all on Mahé, where he lived after the age of 9.[7] René went to a seminary in Switzerland for two years in the 1950s to prepare for the priesthood, but was advised by the church to remain a layman because he did not have "a priestly temperament." He subsequently completed his secondary education at St. Mary's College, Southampton, England, and then went on to earn a law degree from the University of London in 1957. His official biography says that his studies were frequently interrupted because of "financial difficulties" and that he often had to work during the day and study in the evening. Those who knew him during the period of his education suggest that he was not nearly so badly off as he now claims.[8]

René returned to the Seychelles in 1958 for almost three years, but then went back to study at the London School of Economics for more than two years (1961–1964). While in England, René was an active member of the Labour party; he has said that the experience gave him "the chance to study practical politics."[9] Returning again to the Seychelles, René bought a piece of property on Mahé's highest peak, Morne Seychellois, in an area that now sits in the middle of a national forest. The fact that he got the property so cheaply, and that he purchased it just before the government banned the sale of property in the area, attests to his shrewdness, his business sense, and his potential influence in the eyes of the British. Using funds earned as a lawyer, and as prime minister and subsequently president of Seychelles, René has built for himself a home on Morne Seychellois that is often considered to be the finest on any of the islands.

René is not known for prudery in his private life, but he has purposely tried to create quite a different public impression for himself than did his predecessor. His picture regularly appears on the front page of *Nation* – the government-owned newspaper and the only daily allowed to be printed – but it is always in connection with some constructive civic activity like snipping opening-day ribbons or addressing gatherings. He frequently travels out of the Seychelles – he has recently been to China, Europe, Tanzania, Libya, Algeria, Cuba, South Korea, and India – but on all such occasions he argues that pressure of work prevents him from doing much touring, taking part in any kind of night life, or otherwise relaxing. In private conversation he often likens himself and the people around him to Nyerere and his associates, the implication being that his government is not corrupt and is committed to socialist equality.

Among the Seychellois, who are highly politicized, it was originally assumed that René's socialism stemmed in large part from his precoup machinations to secure support from Tanzania. According to this widely held theory, René and his associates had to adopt socialist slogans in order to secure the backing of Tanzania and the OAU, both before and after the coup. As René's regime has pressed ahead with quite radical socialist programs, however, people have been forced to take the government's socialist pretensions more seriously. The consensus – among both friends and enemies of the new government – now seems to be that René and his ministers are not so blatantly corrupt as Mancham's government, are to a man extremely hardworking and dedicated, and are genuinely committed to socialism. It is widely believed that René and some of his ministers may have shared in the general corruption of the Mancham government when they were in coalition with it, but rumors of bribe-taking at high levels are somewhat rarer now than they were under Mancham and there are few visible signs of the kinds of petty corruption that directly involves the public in most of the Third World. In contrast to most African and Asian countries, there is relatively little or no bureaucratic delay, as most rules are known and enforced.

Ever since the coup, Mancham has been exiled in England, where he and conservative British interests have launched a steady barrage of criticism at René's government. Mancham's people insist (with some justification) that they were already planning many of the welfare programs and other reforms that René has now claimed as his own; they are unequivocally opposed to the new government's more radical socialist measures and its suppression of political dissidents. The need for at least a period of adjustment to the new government on the part of old-line Britishers and Anglophiles is understandable. British culture and economic interests had been growing steadily in the Seychelles during the past century, and Mancham's regime had promised extremely close ties between Victoria and London. Even after he came out for independent nationhood, Mancham still sported the Union Jack on his party flag. Moreover, Mancham's SDP had always identified with some of the most conservative British political traditions; its counsel to followers on election posters in 1974 was "Don't lose your head; don't vote Red."[10]

Mancham publicly labeled the 1977 coup "a Soviet-backed invasion" and "part and parcel of the Soviet policy of controlling the Indian Ocean."[11] Mancham supporters point out that the Soviet Embassy had opened in Victoria just four days before the coup, that the Soviet mission subsequently expanded to more than three dozen families in 1981, and that TASS is now the only international news service resident on the islands, being located in the same building as *Nation* and Seychelles Radio. The conspicuous presence in Victoria of Soviet transport vehicles and weapons for the army is also viewed by Mancham as concrete evidence of Soviet backing for the new government.

Seychelles officials do not deny they are receiving weapons and other assistance from Moscow, but they argue that, in contrast to Mancham's pro-Western orientation, they are simply nonaligned. Charges in the British press in 1978 that the Soviets were negotiating for a naval base on one of the outer islands were vigorously denied. René used the occasion to reaffirm his government's official support of the idea that the Indian Ocean should be a "zone of peace," although he also stated that "warships of all nations will continue to be welcome in the Seychelles . . . so long as they do not attempt to interfere in our affairs."[12] René has since made it known that he has rejected Soviet offers to establish a Soviet-controlled fishing industry on Mahé, preferring instead to deal with the French and British. The desire on the part of the government to involve both the British and French in the development of fishing is perhaps the strongest indication that it is seeking a position of genuine nonalignment.

THE 1979 CONSTITUTION

The first constitution of the Seychelles, which was drafted at the end of British rule and remained in effect less than a year after independence, provided for a British-style prime minister and parliament, with full protection of human rights guaranteed by courts empowered to declare void any law that infringed those rights. The constitution was abrogated immediately following the 1977 coup d'etat. René then ruled by presidential proclamation and ordinance for two years while the Constitutional Commission he appointed drafted a new constitution. René's six-person Constitutional Commission was headed by Dr. P. Telford Georges, a noted jurist from the West Indies, and was composed of four people close to René plus Bernard Verlaque, editor and publisher of the newspaper *Weekend Life* (who was later twice arrested by René and eventually forced into exile from the islands because of his persistent defense of civil liberties and a free press).

The Georges Commission considered sixty-eight memorandums submitted to it, of which thirty positively recommended establishment of a one-party state and three emphatically rejected it. The majority of the memorandums (thirty-five of the sixty-eight) accepted the widespread feeling that a one-party monopoly was inevitable and tried simply to influence the drafting of specific clauses. The Constitutional Commission gave only a single reason for recommending a one-party state — that it would "end factional strife" — and rejected a recommendation made in many of the memorandums that a referendum be held to determine whether the Seychellois themselves would vote for one-partyism.[13] Rejection of the referendum idea was a direct consequence of an evaluation by René and his associates that the electorate would overwhelmingly reject one-party rule; the official reason for rejecting it was that the one-party state could not be adequately defined for purposes of a vote because of "the confusion surrounding the term," with the result that a referendum "would not be meaningful."[14]

Figure 3.4. The Constitutional Commission that drafted the 1979 constitution. The three men visible on the left are Bernard Verlaque, who was exiled from the Seychelles in early 1980 because of his objections to the one-party state and censorship of the press; Jacques Hodoul, now Foreign Minister and the leading Marxist theoretician of the SPPF government; and P. Telford Georges of the West Indies, Chairman of the Seychelles Constitutional Commission. Courtesy Seychelles Agence Press.

The commission conceded that its proposed one-party state would impose limits on fundamental rights—freedom of association, speech, and press, for example—but it insisted that all such freedoms must be "subject to the general welfare." To avoid factional conflict and "in light of the realities of the political situation of the Seychelles today," the commission argued, "it will be in the general welfare of the society that the limitation of [fundamental rights] be accepted."[15] In the 1979 constitution, which came into effect on 5 June 1979, therefore, a long list of human rights is described simply as "the intention of the People of Seychelles," with no provision being made to guarantee them.[16] Some rights are significantly qualified (for example, the right to property is championed only to the extent that it is "not inconsistent with the institution and development of a socialist system"), the courts have been stripped of their power of judicial review, and a separate law has made it illegal "to form or to attempt to form any political party other than the Seychelles People's Progressive Front . . . or to engage in political activity except under the auspices of the Front."

Not only is the SPPF specifically mentioned in the 1979 constitution as the only legitimate political party, the party's constitution is even explicitly included as Schedule 2 of the national constitution. From the

perspective of the Georges Commission, the purpose of the 1979 constitution was to establish the SPPF as "the single fount of political
authority." Candidates for elections to the People's Assembly can only be
nominated by district branch offices of the SPPF and can be vetoed only
by the SPPF Central Executive Committee. The 1979 elections were held
on the basis of universal adult franchise and there were two or more candidates in nineteen of the twenty-three constituencies, but all fifty-five of
the candidates for the twenty-three seats were, by constitutional fiat,
members and nominees of the SPPF.[17]

Judicial review was rejected by the Georges Commission because
"there would be the real risk of creating a confrontation between the
judiciary and a united political authority from which neither is likely to
emerge without damage."[18] The commission, therefore, stated flatly that
"if oppressive laws are passed, the Courts will have to apply them." The
only safeguard against oppressive laws, said the commission, "is
widespread political participation to ensure that laws of that character
are not passed."

Although some legislative powers are vested in the People's
Assembly, the legislature is clearly subservient to the party and the
president, with the president being the unquestioned leader of the party.
The president must report to the Assembly once a year, but he can call it
into session or prorogue it virtually at will and none of its bills become
law unless he signs them. Its principal purpose is to enact into law proposals presented by the executive. Representatives of the People's
Assembly are elected every four years, but the president has a five-year
term, the seemingly facetious comment of the commission on this clause
being that "the need for change at the local level may be felt more rapidly
than the need for change in national leadership."[19] The Assembly has a
Public Accounts Committee, which does not have access to all the accounts in the president's office; there are no other legislative committees.
Committees on health, agriculture, education, and so forth are located in
the political party rather than the legislature, the reasoning of the Constitutional Commission being that people should be encouraged to join
the SPPF rather than the legislature if they want to influence or for-
mulate public policy.

The president can appoint and fire ministers and all other public or
party officials, virtually at his pleasure. If a People's Assembly representative is appointed a minister, he or she must resign from the Assembly,
thus eliminating the possibility that a minister might build an electoral
base from which to challenge the president. The president appoints the
chief justice and, in consultation with the chief justice, all other judges.
The president can remove the chief justice and all other judges if a three-
person tribunal, which the president appoints, proves charges of miscon-

duct against the judge. There are a Complaints Office and an Integrity Commission, but both are powerless because they are appointed by the president at his pleasure and have "no right to insist on being given information or on being shown files." The Public Service Commission, which existed under the previous government to provide a safeguard against political interference in administration, was abolished with the 1979 constitution because, in the words of the Georges Commission, "in the one-party state the concept of neutrality has no logical place. . . . The senior civil servant can and should identify with the single party."[20]

The president of the Seychelles is head of state and commander-in-chief of the armed forces and has virtually unlimited constitutional powers. He is nominated by the National Congress of the SPPF and is formally elected on the basis of universal adult franchise in elections in which no other presidential candidates are allowed (in the June 1979 election President René received 26,390 votes—98 percent of the total—with only 541 voters daring to vote against him).[21] He has appointed and can fire the nine ministers in his Council of Ministers, who do not have to be approved by the People's Assembly. The justification for this procedure was that "today, technical competence of Ministers is the overriding consideration and, accordingly, the President should have a free hand in choosing his team without any possible compromises that approval by the People's Assembly might involve."[22] Ministers can attend and speak in the Assembly but they cannot vote in it. The president, all the ministers and all members of the People's Assembly are exempt from criminal or judicial proceedings. The attorney general is appointed and fired by the president; he is not subject to the direction or control of any other person or authority.

THE SPPF

The SPPF is essentially René's creation. René is described by those who have known him over the years as someone who has always been extremely ambitious, highly idealistic, always willing to fight against anyone in authority over him, and often on the side of the black Creole population. Many Seychellois attribute René's chip-on-the-shoulder attitude toward life to his presumed status as an illegitimate child, which caused him to be subjected to fairly constant teasing as a student and occasionally thwarted his aspirations to upper-class respectability. Although such psychological hypotheses are unlikely to be tested with adequate data, René himself has frequently discussed his early years in similar terms. He has often been quoted as saying, for example, that "as a child I was poor. I was always against the system and I always wanted to change it."[23] In 1978 he spoke informally to a party meeting as follows:

> I came back to Seychelles as a lawyer in 1958 and spent three years in
> Seychelles [before going off for two more years in England]. In those three
> years . . . I discovered that if you wanted to get on you had to belong to the
> upper class. And you had to be careful with whom you mixed. As a profes-
> sional I was not supposed to rub shoulders too much with the middle class
> and I was not supposed to rub shoulders at all with the working class.[24]

For whatever reason, René identified strongly with an older lawyer
named Charles Collet who, as acting attorney general in the Seychelles in
the early 1950s, was subjected to considerable harassment by the
Seychelles Taxpayers' and Producers' Association (STPA) because of his
attempts to regularize income-tax regulations and collect back taxes on
behalf of Selwyn-Clarke's "socialist" colonial government. Collet's run-ins
with the *grands blancs* made headlines in England and were discussed on
a number of occasions in the British Parliament. At that time, allegations
were made that racial discrimination was "the actual if unnamed issue" in
an extortion case brought against Collet by STPA, Collet being a black
Seychellois with African and Indian blood who had married a white
Frenchwoman.[25] More than a quarter century after the Collet incident,
René recollected that period as follows:

> I remember . . . joining the Seychelles Club at the instigation of other
> members of the bar and I recollect the trouble I had because I happened in
> those days to be a close friend of Charles Collet. . . . Because I was a friend
> of his and because he did not have the right standing in society, I was
> castigated and very often I had fights in the Seychelles Club. As a result, a
> few days after having been accepted as a member, I resigned.[26]

René described his early professional years as a time when "certain
members of the judiciary tried to get me into the same sort of trouble that
Charles Collet got into." He talked of threats of disbarment, machinations by Supreme Court justices and other judges to prevent him from
contesting elections, and harassment by leading citizens, who paid young
students to stick their heads through the door of his office every morning
and evening for more than three months in a row to taunt him and shout
insults at him. During the period of his rise to political power, René
charged the Mancham government with "intensification of police action
against trade unionists, frame-ups and police investigations, use of police
informers with convictions as many as their years of life, and display of
police dogs at public functions."[27] All of this, René suggested, was
"gradually turning this place into a police state worthy of the South
African influence prevalent here."[28]

René's first political party, SPUP, was founded in 1963, the same
year as Mancham's SDP, with the manifestos of both, in the words of one

political leader of the day, being "full of printing errors and idealism."
Elections in the Seychelles had been introduced only in 1948; universal
adult franchise came with the 1967 elections. By that time, René's SPUP
had organized the first trade union strike in the history of the Seychelles
and had begun to conduct campaigns with a gloves-off style never before
witnessed on the islands. Describing the electoral campaigns of 1967 and
1970, a South African observer noted that "politics had come to the
Seychelles late, but with a vengeance. . . . In fact, the occasional bombing
incident has become an ugly feature of the islands' politics."[29]

In the early election campaigns in the Seychelles, René's SPUP was
not averse to using race as a means of picking up support from the black
Creole population, and at times SPUP attacks on the government
bordered on racism. Mancham, for example, was described by the SPUP
weekly *The People* as "a Chinaman . . . [whose] flirtations with Formosa
. . . are well-known."[30] An editorial written by René in the same year
threatened that "the people of Seychelles . . . will one day somehow or
other kick out the British, *kick out the Indians* and kick out all those who
have not realized that the Seychelles belong to the Seychellois."[31] In his
election campaigns, René often described Mancham as "a stupid stooge"
and Mancham's SDP as "a desperate and shaky gang" who were trying "to
make the people of Seychelles believe that in spite of their skins they
should hate Africa."[32] SPUP was always depicted in highly moral
terms—as a party trying to modernize the black Seychellois population—while Mancham was painted as a "bootlicker of the imperialists"
who wanted blacks to maintain their "slavish mentality." In 1971, for example, René wrote:

> . . . what are Mancham's beliefs? The people believe in God—so feed them
> with inventions about the destruction of their churches. The people believe
> in gris-gris—so give them more gris-gris. . . . The people love drinking—so
> give them drinks and bring in hippies with drugs. The people love sex—so
> advertise proudly the sexual prowess of the Seychellois. And if a warship
> comes in, let the sailors not face a lack of girls. Call them down over Radio
> Seychelles for fun and games, music and dancing, drinking and merry-
> making. This is Mancham! This is opportunism.[33]

Two key figures who have been with René from the early years of
his political career are Ogilvie Berlouis, minister of internal affairs in the
first postcoup government and then defense minister, and Guy Sinon,
originally foreign minister and then minister for administration and
political organization. Sinon is nearing the end of his political career
because of ill health (he suffered a stroke in May 1981), but both he and
Berlouis were important in establishing the new government because of
their extensive contacts in East Africa. Berlouis was the SPUP's represen-

tative in Tanzania until a month before the coup and played a major role in the military operations that resulted in René's assumption of power. Sinon was with the British army in Uganda for a number of years and had helped organize migrant Seychellois youth in SPUP trade unions throughout East Africa before the coup.

The chief Marxist theoretician of the SPPF is Jacques Hodoul, minister of education and culture for the first three years of the new government and then foreign minister. Hodoul was at one time a priest, later a London-trained practicing lawyer; he is, in addition, a trained teacher with Canadian credentials. He comes from a family of landowners who trace their ancestry to a famous pirate and slave trader of the nineteenth century. As education minister, Hodoul instituted a number of projects designed to inculcate Marxist ideas in the population, including programming on Seychelles Radio of lectures designed by the Education Ministry for use in classrooms and a National Youth Service in which Marxist political education plays a prominent role (see Chapter 4).

Leadership of the SPPF and that of the government are closely intertwined, with René being president of both and eight of René's nine ministers holding all of the important positions in the party. Amid persistent rumors of pro- and anti-Soviet factions among the ministers (Hodoul and Minister of Information James Michel are supposed to be pro-Soviet, with Sinon and Berlouis being anti-Soviet), there was remarkable continuity during the first four years that the SPPF ruled on its own. René added two ministers of state (Karl St. Ange, a former hotel owner from La Digue, who is in charge of agriculture and fisheries, and Esme Jumeau, a former electrical contractor who lived for a number of years in East Africa, in charge of youth and community development). He also reshuffled several ministries in 1981 when it became necessary to relieve the ailing Sinon of the pressures of office. Aside from these few changes, however, the same people who staged the coup in 1977 remained in charge.

Sinon, who has been more responsible for organizing the SPPF than anyone other than René, described a process of evolution in the party after 1977 which he called "a move for quality and not simply quantity."[34] Rather than recruit primarily people who could stage demonstrations or contest elections, he says, the party decided that it needed "leaders . . . who would be committed and more far-sighted in delivering to the people the fruits of liberation." Sinon and others, therefore, formulated the idea of converting the SPUP, which they had previously envisaged as an electoral party operating in a liberal democratic state, into the SPPF, which they call a "socialist avant garde Party." The basic idea behind the change was to establish Leninist-style democratic centralist lines of authority, in order to better enable the party's leadership to become the

Figure 3.5. Leaders of the Seychelles People's Progressive Front (SPPF), the only legal political party on the islands. The 9 men between the woman on the right and the man on the far left are also 9 of the 10 ministers in the Seychelles government. Photo courtesy Seychelles Agence Press.

"avant-garde" of the proletariat within the framework of a one-party state.

The change in the SPUP from a liberal democratic to an authoritarian party is the most striking feature of contemporary Seychelles politics. Whereas René promised in radio broadcasts before independence that "I would never use violence to get the support of anyone" and his party championed freedom of expression, freedom of association, and an independent civil service "not under the control of a political Government," the successor party to SPUP has completely shifted away from such a stance.[35] SPPF General-Secretary Sinon has explained this shift as follows:

> I would say today that [seeking power through elections] was a tactical move in the sense that it helped us to see how things were working from the inside . . . and was in the interest of national unity. But something had to happen, something needed to be done. We had to move for total liberation. So we decided to take up arms to abolish the status quo.[36]

Party leaders have argued that denial of some civil liberties was and is necessary to establish discipline in the country and to end factional strife; lack of party competition in national elections is supposed to be compensated for by intraparty elections at the local and national level. The party is now organized into twenty-three branches, each branch coinciding with a constituency for the People's Assembly. The way to rise in the party is to get elected to the Executive Committee of the branch, with party elections being held by secret ballot at the local level every year. All adults over the age of 16 are expected to become members of the SPPF and to pay monthly dues and an admission fee. It is from among the most active and those who are most encouraged by the central leadership of the party that local party leaders are ultimatel chosen.

Party funds come from membership dues (the chief coordinator of the party, Sylvette Frishot, claimed in mid-1981 that the party had more than 8,000 members), from domestic and international contributions, from the sale of party publications, and from its front groups. The new SPPF headquarters—in a beautiful, newly constructed building near the port—was paid for by a grant to the party from Algeria; it was furnished in part by contributions from businessmen and other donors. Liberal contributions to the SPPF have also come from Libya and the Soviet bloc. The sale of party publications is guaranteed by the absence in the bookstores of any other publications for learning about crucial political decisions. The National Workers Union, the only trade union allowed in the country, is listed in the party constitution as an official "front group" and receives 25 percent of the total contributions for union membership dues from all workers in the country. These funds, plus occasional income from party-run lotteries, picnics, and other social events, are sufficient to maintain a fairly extensive permanent party staff and two other party front organizations (the National Women's Organisation and the National Youth Organisation). The women's and youth organizations do not charge dues. Membership in the women's organization is more or less required of good female party members. The National Youth Organisation consists of two subsidiary party training organizations—the Young Pioneers (ages 6–12) and the Pioneers (ages 12–16). In 1981 the two youth organizations together had approximately 2,000 members.

One of the most striking aspects of the SPPF since 1977 has been the way in which it has brought a number of women into leadership positions, particularly at the branch level. There are no women in René's Council of Ministers, but nine of the twenty-five members of the People's Assembly (two of the twenty-five are appointed, not elected) and a majority (twelve of twenty-three) of the party's branch chairmen are women. Most of these women, as well as most other branch chairmen, are from middle-class and managerial families and almost all of them are fairly well educated. Although precise data on their socioeconomic backgrounds are not available, most of them would appear to be in their 30s and 40s, active in social welfare and school activities in their localities, and otherwise representative of a new wave of upwardly mobile and ambitious "solid citizens" who have benefited from the postairport economic boom of the 1970s.

René and the SPUP have frequently been objects of derision by many people in the upper class in Seychelles because the party, from the beginning, exhibited a number of contradictions. It called itself a liberal democratic party and championed a Westminster-type parliamentary government, yet it aspired to socialism in support of the poor. It was led predominantly by middle-class professionals, managers, smaller businessmen, landowners, and teachers, but it adopted slogans and tactics appealing to lower-class laborers and unemployed "rowdies." As the party in power since 1977, the SPUP (now the SPPF) has not carried out an extensive and consistent land reform, although it has nationalized the estates of some of its political opponents and is trying to establish state farms.

Prior to the coup of 5 June 1977, Mancham, the larger business classes, and the *grands blancs* all tended to minimize their differences with René and the SPUP, as indicated by Mancham's willingness to allow René to remain in charge of the government as prime minister while Mancham traveled extensively abroad. The coup was, therefore, a shock to Seychellois society. Not only did it introduce a politics of weapons and violence for the first time to a country that had never previously had an army, it also indicated that René and his associates could be quite ruthless in pursuit of their goals.

Even after the coup, there was a wistful hope on the part of some members of the Seychelles establishment that the coup had been a temporary (and perhaps even necessary) aberration and that René's government would settle down to something resembling the gentlemanly politics of the past. A number of convulsions since—including the nationalization of all medical facilities, the establishment of the highly politicized and ideological National Youth Service, the suppression of civil liberties, and the occasional use of terror and coercion to punish or exile dissidents—have convinced both the Seychellois and outside observers that René's revolutionary socialist aspirations are to be taken seriously.

SECURITY CONCERNS

Having come to power by force and with the assistance of Tanzania, René and his government are acutely aware of their own vulnerability should a small band of determined Seychellois decide to link up with another foreign army or group of mercenaries. The René government claimed that its defensiveness was justified by the events of the night of 25 November 1981, when a group of about fifty South Africa-based mercenaries, led by 62-year-old Michael Hoare, who had previously helped install Mobutu Sese Seko as president of Zaire, attempted to smuggle themselves and a cache of arms into the Seychelles in preparation for a major coup attempt in early 1982. After the mercenaries were discovered by an alert customs official at the airport, they hijacked an Air India commercial airliner and flew to Durban, where they were arrested by the South African government. The Seychelles government has since accused South Africa of complicity in the coup attempt and has condemned Pretoria for refusing to either extradite the mercenaries or give them severe sentences. President René has also lauded the Soviet Union for its quick response in sending warships to Seychelles waters immediately upon receipt of a request for military aid.[37]

Ever since 1977, rumors have constantly circulated in Victoria about various countercoup attempts that are either being planned or have been planned. For a few years, the most widely accepted rumor was that Mancham and Joubert were using money from wealthy Arabs, who presumably had lost on their investments in the Seychelles because of the 1977 coup, to train foreign mercenaries and Seychellois residents abroad for an attempted countercoup at some opportune time in the future. René himself fed such rumors in November 1978 by stating at a press conference that "some ex-ministers" were living lavishly in London and Australia with money from a source that he knew but could not reveal; he went on to say that the ex-ministers "were still dreaming that they would come back to Seychelles and were still talking about the formation of clubs and organizations in order to try and come back." Speaking of Joubert specifically, René said: "I think that he will end up an old man still dreaming that he should be back here, because you must bear in mind that someone like him has nothing else he can do; even if he wanted to work he could do very little and, as a result, he will carry on trying to foment trouble."

In fact, the British diplomat who in 1977 informed Mancham that he was no longer prime minister of the Seychelles said that Mancham, at the time, seemed "greatly relieved" to learn of the coup. Mancham's friends say that he genuinely did not want to govern the Seychelles without the British. Other diplomatic sources suggest that a number of Kenyans and Arabs had planned an intricate countercoup for the Seychelles in late 1977 and early 1978, but those plans collapsed when Mancham refused to give his assent to them. Mancham's reasoning was that a countercoup attempt would inevitably result in considerable bloodshed, and he did not want to assume responsibility for the deaths of his countrymen.

René and his party have used the threat of a countercoup as justification for a number of controversial activities that are hotly debated among Seychellois. For the first time in the country's history the government has amended the Post Office Act in such a way as to allow private mail to be "opened, delayed, intercepted or detained" by the chief postmaster if he believes it "in the interest of the country to do so."[38] The government has also called in all private arms and has established regular military bases on Coetivy Island and at Pointe Larue on Mahé. Some Seychellois are incensed by the calling-in of arms, arguing that the rat and barn owl populations have been increasing geometrically because of lack of weapons among the populace. Conservationists became especially upset about the location of army training exercises in an area that had previously been part of a national marine park or in areas that could be used for agriculture, even though Defense Minister Ogilvie assured them that such areas will be "a showpiece, demonstrating the productivity and self-sufficiency of the young soldiers of the Seychelles."[39]

The most disputed action of the René government has been the promulgation of Public Security Regulations in late April 1978 and the subsequent detention without trial of 21 prominent Seychelles citizens for a period of more than two months in 1978 and the detention of 120 persons for a few days each in late 1979 and early 1980. In arresting the 21 citizens in 1978, René was reacting to reports in a French newspaper that Bob Dénard, a famous French mercenary leader, and a group of 20 white mercenaries were sailing toward the Indian Ocean on the *Masiwa*, a rusting 30-year-old trawler, to stage a coup in one of the island nations. As it turned out, Dénard was successful in overthrowing the government of Ali Soilih in the Comoro Islands, 700 miles (1,100 kilometers) west of Seychelles, on 13 May 1978, replacing Soilih with the less progressive Ahmed Abdullah, a man whom Dénard had previously helped oust.[40] When releasing the 21 detainees in early July 1978, after the Dénard coup was firmly established, René invited his ex-prisoners to leave the country "for another, where they might find the system more to their liking." René also warned the nation at the time that "there might be other people or organizations who will try to overthrow the government."[41]

The arrests of 1979 and 1980 were prompted by a rumor that several highly placed police officers were scheming with the crew of Seychelles' only naval vessel, with backing from groups in France, to overthrow the René regime. Some of those arrested, including Bernard Verlaque, were asked to go into permanent exile from the Seychelles;

most of the others left voluntarily. Fortunately for the dissidents, there are large communities of Seychellois already living in Britain, France, Kenya, and Australia (there are more than 12,000 Seychellois resident in Australia alone), with enough anti-René people living in those communities to assist in finding employment and otherwise arranging for a transfer of residence. Those – including some of the president's most enthusiastic supporters – who disagree with René's conscious policy of exiling his enemies have suggested privately that he may have been a bit paranoid about the possibility of a countercoup. They also question the wisdom of his creating large numbers of vitriolic enemies among Seychellois living abroad.

René admitted that his policy of exiling dissidents may have made them "even more bitter towards us," but he argued that exile is preferable to the harsher methods that might be used. In 1980 he publicly accused dissident Seychellois communities in Australia, Britain, South Africa, and Mauritius of plotting against him and issued "a warning that if we do decide to act against them we will do so with every means at our disposal."[42] To make this threat clearer, René added: "We did not harm any person. Some still retain business interests and other assets here in Seychelles."[43] In 1981 he repeated this threat and added to it, "Either we help with the construction efforts – or else we get out. And if some people are not sufficiently honest to do so by themselves, I, as the President chosen by the people, will ensure that they are made to get out as soon as possible."[44] Referring to a group of students who had protested the establishment of the National Youth Service, René told his Liberation Day audience in June 1981 that "children who cause problems at school will be transferred to a special school. At the same time, we will set up a new institution where those who will not allow others to live in peace can be sent by the courts to undergo a period of reflection and discipline."[45]

Given the introduction of press censorship, a lack of privacy in the mails, the curtailment of judicial freedoms, preventive detention, schools for enforcing political discipline, and forced exile, it is not surprising that an element of fear has been introduced into Seychelles politics. Fears have been fed by a number of instances in which people have simply disappeared from the streets, the most prominent of these being Hassan Ali, owner of a motorcycle repair shop and an outspoken opponent of the new regime. Ali's car and shoes were found on the street one day, but neither his wife nor anyone else has been able to find a trace of him since. A factor further contributing to an atmosphere of fear and suspicion has been the rather wholesale and at times whimsical housecleaning affecting almost every aspect of the administrative structure, including replacement of the chief justice of the Supreme Court, the police chief, the head of the Police Riot Squad, the head of every administrative office, and hundreds of others.

The creation of an army has led to a number of problems with the police, who feel that they have now been made second-class citizens. René has frequently posed with policemen in public and is constantly being quoted about the importance of the police and the need for them to conceive of themselves as "friends of the people." At the same time, René has armed the militia but has refused arms to the police and has expanded the size of the police force by including within its ranks large numbers of female traffic wardens and clerks. Some policemen have been so incensed that several brawls between police and army men have broken out in downtown Victoria, leading to quick public denials by the government that either the police or army was involved. As a sop to the police, René has publicly warned his army officers that they should practice "self-discipline and dignity" as a sign of their "maturity" in order to "demonstrate that they are worthy of the positions they hold in society."[46]

People who know René well suggest that he has not always been as suspicious or as authoritarian as he has become in recent years. A number of them recall his saying years ago that he would never become a politician who kept his doors closed to anyone. Others point out that he always objected to the use of bodyguards, either for himself or for others. Today, René is as shielded from the public as almost any political leader in Africa or Asia; all roads to his home are barred by roadblocks, and a number of woods and peaks have been cleared near his home to provide protection against potential snipers or other terrorists. René's movements are often kept secret or revealed only at the last minute; his office is unapproachable without a prior appointment and several gate checks along the corridors.

THE ARMY AND THE FUTURE

The 1977 coup d'etat in the Seychelles was particularly interesting because it was carried out in a country that did not have an army. In nations where an indigenous military has carried out a coup, experience has shown that civil-military conflicts frequently develop and the military either ends up remaining in power or intervening again when civilian rule breaks down. But what about Seychelles? Is the newly created military strong enough to intervene in politics at some point in the future? Could it conceivably prevent or retard military intervention by other nations? What other roles can it be expected to perform?

The Seychelles People's Militia was established shortly after the 1977 coup, but the core of that army was the sixty Tanzanian-trained guerrillas who had taken up arms against the Mancham government.

Figure 3.6. Seychelles soldiers guarding a crowd at National Stadium. Author's photo.

Since the coup, Tanzanian and Indian officers have played a major role in training the army, which is gradually being expanded toward a planned size of about a thousand men. Tanzanian soldiers were in evidence in Seychelles during the first few months after the coup, but they have since been relegated to behind-the-scenes jobs at army bases, with Seychellois assuming more and more responsibility for public tasks. As mentioned earlier, rifles, troop carriers, and other military equipment have in the past come almost exclusively from the Soviet Union. In 1981 the Libyans indicated their willingness to provide military hardware as well.

The basic structure of the military was established in December 1980, with the enactment of two laws detailing a legal procedure for disciplining soldiers and providing for separate commands for the army, navy, and air force. The principal tasks of the navy and air force have been defined as "maritime defense"—i.e., detecting foreign vessels fishing or otherwise operating in the Seychelles economic maritime zone. The army is obviously intended to maintain domestic order. Soldiers are visibly present in substantial numbers in Victoria whenever a large crowd is expected or the president appears publicly. They can also be seen in their official uniforms—resembling the battle fatigues used on the night of 5 June 1977—conscientiously patrolling key installations like the radio station, the president's office, and the airport.

The first group of soldiers entirely trained by Seychellois officers was turned out in April 1981.[47] At that point, the highest-ranking officer in the Seychelles military was a major, there being no leading officer of any higher rank known to the public except for two ministers who have been given the rank of colonel. The government has been careful to publicize only civilian roles in the coup of 1977, and little or no publicity has been given to any military officer since the coup. The leading figures in the army are Major Raymond Bonté, a close friend and former legal client of President René, Major Phillip Lucas, commanding officer of the military base at Pointe Larue, and Major Macdonald Marengo, commander of the training camp on Coetivy Island. The head of the navy, which has one ship under its command, is Captain Paul Hodoul, brother of the foreign minister. Like the navy, the air force has a single vessel and bears more resemblance to a small club than it does to a larger-scale military establishment.

Most of the members of the Seychelles military have been recruited from among the laboring classes, although the officer corps is increasingly being recruited from middle-class and managerial families. Among the first soldiers were many young men with criminal records who had been purposely recruited by the SPUP because of their knowledge of weapons and their willingness to engage in the guerrilla operations necessary to carry out the coup. Training has been carried out in military skills, building, construction, mechanics, farming, fishing, and political education. According to its own pronouncements, the government rejects the notion that the army should be apolitical or politically neutral, but politicization of the military in this context means simply that "our troops . . . are trained to defend the interests of socialism and to work for the economic and socialist development of the country."[48] In fact, the government has tried to devise a number of ways to keep the military subservient to the government and the party.

President René's attempt to gain control of the military can be seen from the way in which he has relegated administrative responsibility for the Defense Forces to two ministers simultaneously. Ogilvie Berlouis, as minister of defense, also has the title "Chief of the Defense Forces," but the "Chief of Staff of the Defense Forces" is Minister for Education and Information James Michel. Both men are appointed by the president at his pleasure and both report directly to the president, who retains the title of commander-in-chief. Both ministers have been given the status of colonel. It is no coincidence that Michel and Berlouis tend to be in different factional camps and that both have taken a strong interest in military and security affairs since well before the coup. The president is also advised by the Defense Council, which consists primarily of additional knowledgeable civilian defense analysts whom René appoints. A People's Militia, separate from the regular army, has been recruited by the SPPF and given the right to bear arms. In August 1981 the SPPF Annual Congress voted to make all of the People's Defense Forces organizationally part of the SPPF.

As far as possible, René has tried to structure things in such a way that his successor would be elected by the party in the event of his death or incapacity. Constitutionally, René can run for two more five-year terms after his present term expires in 1984. The constitution does not provide for a vice-president, the argument of the Georges Commission being that such an office "would appear to involve an attempt at influencing the choice of a successor, which could be undesirable."[49] If the vice-president was a figurehead, the commission went on to state, "he might well have difficulty in keeping the Government together in the interim period." The process of succession outlined in the constitution provides for the Council of Ministers to elect one of their number to act as president until a single new presidential candidate can be nominated by the party and elected.

The Seychelles military, no matter how strong, could not prevent a takeover by a major power that was prepared to intervene in the nation's politics with force. However, it can prevent or quash smaller interventions by factions of domestic dissidents or foreign mercenaries without significant foreign backing, as it did in November 1981. The obvious danger for governmental leaders is that the military capability they create for the defense of their own regime might well be turned against that regime at some point in the future.

President René has justified the ruthlessness exhibited during his rise to power by pointing to his class background as the son of a plantation manager from one of the poorer and more isolated islands, his argument being that upper-class oppression necessitated the use of violence in defense of lower-class interests. It might be argued that it is precisely from René's social background—the rising middle or managerial class—that one might expect to find the leadership for change in the future. Members of this class tend to be frustrated because they can see and understand the wealth of the upper classes without sharing that wealth, and yet they can also empathize with the oppression of the laboring classes because they sometimes find themselves among the oppressed. In an orderly transition, a future Seychelles president might be expected to come from the leadership ranks of the SPPF, which is composed predominantly of middle-class managers. In the event of another revolutionary upheaval, the leadership of the army—from less establishmentarian backgrounds—is likely to play a major role.

NOTES

1. An excellent account of the coup appears in Michael T. Kaufman, "On Lush Indian Ocean Isles, A Coup Is Just a Hiccup," *New York Times,* June 11, 1977.

2. Christopher Lee, *Seychelles: Political Castaways* (London: Hamish Hamilton, 1976), pp. 148–149. Lee is a British journalist and an admirer of Mancham. More critical of Mancham and René is a book by Australian journalist Athol Thomas, *Forgotten Eden: A View of the Seychelles Islands in the Indian Ocean* (London: Orient Longmans, 1969).

3. An excellent discussion of the constitutional background of Seychelles independence is John M. Ostheimer, "Independence Politics in the Seychelles," in *The Politics of the Western Indian Ocean Islands,* edited by John M. Ostheimer (New York: Praeger Publishers, 1975), pp. 161–192.

4. Lee, *Seychelles,* p. 123.

5. Quoted from an interview in August 1977.

6. *Onward to Socialism: SPPF Policy Statement Adapted at the Second Congress of the Seychelles People's United Party, 31st May to 2nd June, 1978* (Victoria: Government Press, 1978), p. 57.

7. A short biography of René appears in *Weekend Life* (Victoria), Vol. 1, no. 16 (October 15, 1977), p. 8.

8. René's official biography appears in F. A. René, *Philosophy of a Struggle* (Victoria: SPPF, 1977), pp. 35–37.

9. France Albert René, *The Torch of Freedom: A Collection of Speeches and Writings by France Albert René, 1964–1977* (Victoria: Ministry of Education and Information, 1981), p. 11.

10. For a sympathetic view of the Mancham regime by an Anglo-Indian journalist, see Darryl D'Monte, "Seychelles: A Thousand Miles from Anywhere," *Illustrated Weekly of India,* September 12, 1976, pp. 25–29. See also Darryl D'Monte, "A Country Harassed by Continental Problems," *Times of India* (Bombay), September 12, 1976.

11. Quoted in an extensive unsigned summary article in the *Los Angeles Times,* March 24, 1978.

12. The zone of peace pronouncement appears in the *Times of India,* August 9, 1978. The quote is from *Lettre des Seychelles* (monthly review), August 1978, p. 4.

13. A discussion of the referendum issue appears in *Weekend Life,* Vol. 2, nos. 29–31 (January 13 and 26, 1979, and February 3 and 10, 1979).

14. *Charting Our Course: Report of the Constitutional Commission to President F. A. René and Draft Instructions,* Chairman P. Telford Georges (Victoria: Government Press, 1978), p. 2.

15. Ibid.

16. See *Constitution of the Republic of Seychelles Decree, 1979 (No. 14 of 1979)* (Victoria: Government Press, 26 March 1979), pp. 70–73.

17. A list of the candidates appears in *Weekend Life,* Vol. 2, no. 49 (June 16, 1979), p. 6. In the elections to the People's Assembly, the local branch of the SPPF was allowed to nominate up to three candidates in each constituency, with no

other candidates being allowed to contest the elections.

18. All quotes in this paragraph are from *Charting Our Course*, pp. 4–5.

19. Ibid., p. 10.

20. Ibid., p. 13.

21. *Weekend Life*, Vol. 2, no. 51 (June 30, 1979), p. 1.

22. *Charting Our Course*, p. 8.

23. *Weekend Life*, Vol. 1, no. 15 (October 8, 1977), p. 3.

24. Quoted in *Onward to Socialism*, p. 1.

25. The Collet case is detailed in Alec Waugh, *Where the Clocks Chime Twice* (London: Cassell and Company, 1952), pp. 158ff.

26. *Onward to Socialism*, p. 2.

27. Quoted in *The People* (SPUP weekly), November 15, 1972.

28. Ibid.

29. Douglas Alexander, *Holiday in Seychelles: A Guide to the Islands* (Capetown: Purnell Publishers, 1972), p. 34.

30. *The People*, February, 24, 1971.

31. Ibid. Italics added. The fact that this editorial was reprinted in 1981, in René, *Torch of Freedom*, p. 43–45, caused many members of the Indian community, who see themselves as Seychellois, considerable nervousness.

32. Quoted in René, *Torch of Freedom*, pp. 43, 56.

33. Ibid., pp. 49–50.

34. Guy Sinon, "The Struggle for Liberation – The Early Days," *The People* (SPPF monthly), June 1981, p. 5.

35. All quotes and references in this paragraph, unless otherwise noted, are from speeches appearing in *Torch of Freedom*, pp. 34, 39, 76.

36. Sinon, "Struggle for Liberation," pp. 3–4.

37. Extensive coverage of the November 1981 attempted coup appeared in the *International Herald Tribune* in late November and early December. See especially the article by Bernd Debusmann in the issue of December 9, 1981. See also Allister Sparks, "Seychelles and Mercenaries," *Rand Daily Mail* (Johannesburg), December 11, 1981.

38. Details of the amendment appear in *Weekend Life*, Vol. 1, no. 15 (October 14, 1978), p. 1.

39. Ibid., Vol. 1, no. 18 (November 4, 1978), p. 5.

40. The coup in the Comoros is discussed in David Lamb, "Comoros: A Path to Democracy," *International Herald Tribune*, October 21–22, 1978, p. 8. See also "Exit Mercenaries," *India Today* (New Delhi), November 16–30, 1978, pp. 55–57.

41. *Lettre des Seychelles*, August 1978, p. 6.

42. *Nation*, Souvenir Issue, June 5, 1980, p. 41.

43. Ibid.

44. France Albert René, "Discipline and Responsibility," *Nation*, Souvenir Issue, June 5, 1981, p. 9.

45. Ibid.

46. *Nation*, December 11, 1980.

47. Ibid., April 13, 1981, pp. 1–2.

48. Ibid., June 19, 1981, p. 2.

49. *Charting Our Course*, pp. 7–8.

4

Economy

Three decades ago Victoria, the capital of Seychelles, could be described as "a sordid and graceless slum," with "ramshackle, tumbledown shops and shanties" and "a characteristic odor of rancid coconut oil, dried fish and bad drains."[1] The only way to get to Victoria was by ship — six days from Bombay or three from Mombasa — and ships would invariably be met in the harbor by tiny, ramshackle "bum-boats" full of lagoon hawkers trying to sell their baskets of curios, tortoise shells, necklaces, and fruit. The change that came over the port in the 1960s and 1970s was indicated in a South African tourist guidebook published in 1972, in which the author admitted that "Victoria was once virtually all slum — almost the dreariest seaport in the Indian Ocean — and a place to get out of fast." The same author quickly went on to argue that it has now changed so drastically as to be "only a trifle tatty" and "by no means dullsville."[2]

Change began in 1963, when the United States leased a portion of the main island of Mahé and began to build an airforce satellite tracking station. More than one hundred Americans were assigned on a continuous basis to construction teams in the Seychelles in the 1960s, and they brought with them their large cars, electronic gadgets, and a style of living entirely foreign to the Indian Ocean. They also brought regular air travel to the islands for the first time, in the form of a German Albatross seaplane that had previously made occasional flights to the Seychelles but now began a weekly shuttle service between Mombasa and Victoria.

The opening up of air communications with Africa led to a number of demands on Seychelles politicians to build an airport, and it also made clear the vast tourism potential of the islands. Led by Mancham, the government of Seychelles, still under British rule, built a US $12 million airport in 1971, invited foreign capital in to develop hotels and other parts of the tourist industry, started construction on a new port (in which bum-boats are no longer allowed), and set about to remodel all the old shantylike structures in downtown Victoria. By 1980 the number of tourists coming to Seychelles had climbed to almost 73,000 for the year, a more than forty-four fold increase over the 1,622 tourists who came in 1970.

TOURISM

The first effect of the decision to build an airport and develop a tourist industry was a large-scale construction boom in the early 1970s – fueled by unprecedented foreign investments – with construction accounting for as much as 45 percent of growth of gross domestic product (GDP) in 1971 (at that time agriculture accounted for 23 percent of GDP growth and tourism 21 percent).[3] As construction has leveled off in the late 1970s, tourism has increased in importance; in 1978 it accounted for 47 percent of growth in GDP (agriculture remained at 20 percent and construction was down to 24 percent). In 1977 the tourist industry had gross receipts of more than US$45 million – almost half of total imports – and had contributed heavily to other receipts (from use of ports, net investment income, and aid and trade programs).[4] National planners of all persuasions have been quick to recognize that tourism was almost entirely responsible for Seychelles' rather comfortable foreign exchange position in the 1970s and for its ability to remain only marginally behind employment demands.

Tourism has also been the major dynamo producing an incomparable degree of inflation in the Seychelles in the 1970s and 1980s. Prior to the 1960s the islands were known as a place where an old British civil servant or missionary could retire very cheaply, with the most expensive hotel rooms (at the Northolme, for example) being let out at Rs.300 (US $48) *per month*. Today, a bed-and-breakfast *single* at the Northolme is priced at Rs.480 (US $74) *per day* and a room for less than Rs.170 (US $27) per day anywhere, on any of the islands, is difficult to find.

The extent of inflation in the 1970s was heavily influenced by a decision by the government to encourage only the most affluent tourists. Plans devised in the early 1970s were to provide for 100,000 tourists per year by 1982, based on an average 65 percent occupancy and ten-day lengths of stay. The hope of the government was to limit licenses for beds to something like 4,000 only by 1982, restricting annual growth to 10 percent or less. Hygienic and health standards for hotels, restaurants, and guest houses have been rigorously delineated and are scrupulously enforced. To encourage the upper-middle-class tourist from Europe, high-priced group tours are allowed but charter flights and heavily discounted tours are not. No tourist is permitted to sleep overnight on any beach without permission from the police; violations of drug laws carry stiff penalties.

TABLE 4.1

Tourist Statistics, 1971-1980

	No. of Visitor Arrivals	Avg. Length of Stay (nights)	Purpose of Visit*	
			Holiday or Business Holiday (%)	Transit/ Other (%)
1971	3,175	28.5		
1972	15,197	13.1		
1973	19,464	10.5		
1974	25,932	10.2		
1975	37,321	11.1		
1976	49,498	11.5		
1977	54,490	11.0	90.6	9.4
1978	64,995	9.6	88.4	11.6
1979	78,852	9.1	87.2	12.8
1980	72,762	9.0	86.0	14.0

*No statistics exist before 1977.

Source: Republic of Seychelles, Statistical Bulletin, Fourth Quarter, 1980, Vol. 1, no. 3 (Victoria: Government Printers, February 1981), pp. 6-7.

Table 4.1 details the manner in which tourism in the Seychelles grew steadily and at a brisk pace until 1979, when it reached a crest of almost 79,000 visitors. Had that pace of growth continued into the 1980s, the government's planned target of 100,000 visitors by 1982 would have been reached. However, tourist statistics for 1980 and 1981 have been most discouraging, and projections for the next few years do not indicate a likely reversal of recent trends. The official figures indicate that visitor arrivals dropped to less than 73,000 in 1980 and were likely to fall to as few as 55,000 in 1981. Instead of 4,000 beds available, there are only 2,500, and most of these remain empty most of the time. Tourist agents and hotel owners argue that the decline in tourism has been even more severe than official figures would indicate, as the average length of stay of each tourist has been steadily dwindling while the percentage of transit passengers (as opposed to bona fide tourists) has jumped from 9.4 percent in 1977 to 14 percent in 1980 (see Table 4.1).

The decline in Seychelles tourism is in part related to the increased costs of air travel that followed in the wake of the oil-price hikes of the 1970s; it also reflects a decline in real incomes in most of the developed countries, a phenomenon that has hurt tourism world wide. Considering these factors alone, one might argue that the Seychelles survived the first few years of the oil-price hikes because it was a novelty for the jet set during a period when the impact of rapidly escalating oil prices was only gradually being felt by international travelers. But all these explanations fail to fully account for the precipitous drop-off in the numbers of

Seychelles tourists in 1980 and 1981. Additional reasons commonly given for the decline are (1) the Seychelles have been very poorly advertised as a tourist site since Mancham was ousted in the 1977 coup; (2) bad publicity (the coup, internal repression, the forced exiles of 1978 and 1979, and the abortive coup of November 25, 1981) has given Seychelles a poor image, particularly in Europe; (3) identification with black Africa and revolutionary socialism has been distasteful to many potential upper-middle-class tourists from South Africa and Western Europe, two major markets for Seychelles tourism; (4) the pervasive presence of the army—on beaches and streets, in hotels, at the post office, and elsewhere—has turned away potential tourism promoters; and (5) the Seychelles tourist industry has been offering the tourist decreasing value for money spent.

The government has, in its own way, tried to promote tourism and encourage foreigners to invest in tourist enterprises in the Seychelles, but with much less enthusiasm than had been generated under Mancham. Several of the tourist bureaus that Mancham opened abroad were closed, and all Seychelles diplomats abroad were permanently recalled in 1979, both actions being viewed as necessary economy measures despite their adverse effects on promotional activities in tourist market areas. Several tourist establishments (including the Pirates Arms and Northolme Hotel) were nationalized in 1981, and a number of investors who had signed contracts with the Mancham government—including the late Peter Sellers, Hyatt House, Beatle George Harrison, and Prince Talal (brother of King Khaled of Saudi Arabia), who was commited to build a US$30 million Acapulco-type gambling casino at Port Launnay—terminated their agreements after 1977. Government spokesmen say that they are "realistic" and are not consciously discouraging South Africans, but daily diatribes in the government-monopoly Seychelles press against the injustices of apartheid have unquestionably had an adverse effect on that market. An additional inhibiting factor has been government unwillingness to allow sex or any other "undignified" symbols to be associated with Seychelles tourist promotions, preferring instead that travel agents emphasize, in the words of Tourism Minister Mathew Servina, "how we live and the various aspects of our economy and social development."[5]

President René and his ministers refuse to admit that the coup or their policies since have had anything to do with the drop in tourism; instead they argue that the poor health of the Seychelles economy resulting from the decline only "underlines the fragility of too much reliance on tourism."[6] Some travel agents and hotel owners in the Seychelles have recommended to the government that a complete reevaluation of policies regarding tourism be undertaken, but thus far the Tourism Ministry has held out no such possibility. Others are hoping that a recently introduced Air India flight from Salisbury, Zimbabwe, and a new Royal Swazi Air flight will bring back the South Africans, who dropped out in the largest numbers when Air Malawi canceled its flights shortly after the coup. A sure sign of the government's lack of interest in tourism is the fact that less than 1 percent of planned expenditures in the 1980–1984 development plan have been allocated to the Tourism Ministry, as compared with 34 percent for agriculture, fisheries and land development, 28 percent for education, housing, health and youth, and 25 percent for police, administration, information, water and electricity.

TRADE DEFICITS AND FOOD

From a purely economic point of view, tourism was the savior of the Seychelles in the 1970s because it made up more than half the trade deficits incurred in the entire decade. These huge deficits—of a magnitude of twenty to one or greater—are in part the result of a clear preference by the Seychellois for imported foods and consumer goods. It was with this in mind that President René told his countrymen in his 1981 budget address not to rely so much on tourism but instead to initiate campaigns to eliminate "in the minds of our people the evil mentality of preference for imported consumer goods." As many observers have pointed out, René's plea simply repeats what rulers of Seychelles have been asking since the country was last self-sufficient in food in 1834.

Much of the traditional unwillingness of the Seychellois to produce food indigenously is a consequence of the easy living that results from an abundance of fish in the ocean and coconuts in the trees. Large-scale tourism has strengthened the tenacity of this attitude; it has proved to be such an extremely lucrative foreign exchange and income-earner for those involved in it that it has tended to attract most of the educated youth on the islands.

Resulting stereotypes of Seychelles society today are of fast drivers in Japanese cars playing loud music on their tapedecks, of little shanty homes with smoke and jazz emanating from them in the morning and evening hours, or of young women wearing fancy clothes made in London, Paris, and South Africa. Drunkenness—from overconsumption of *bacca* (fermented sugarcane juice) or *calou* (palm toddy)—remains a major social problem, as it has been for the last century, but vastly increased consumption of imported wines and an excellent domestic beer (produced by Guinness) have added to the problem in the 1970s and 1980s. Benedict's studies showed that most Seychellois subsisted in the 1960s on a diet of rice (all of which is imported), plus cassava, plantains, yams and breadfruit, much of which is also imported.[7] Consumption of processed foods has increased manyfold since Benedict's studies. Recent government figures show that the food import bill doubled between 1970 and 1975 and again between 1975 and 1979, accounting throughout this period for more than 20 percent of imports, with almost all of the food coming from South Africa.[8] The country now imports most of its beef, milk, and other dairy products, as well as many fruits and vegetables, flour, sugar, canned goods, and frozen foods.

Domestic meat is provided by pigs and chickens that are raised as backyard scavengers and by octopus, fish, and a highly prized indigenous fruit bat. The Seychellois eat few vegetables, use little bread, and drink less milk than most other peoples; they do consume large quantities of what they call *brèdes* – soups made of green leaves – and chutneys made from green mangoes or apples. Unlike in most parts of Asia and Africa, there is no scavenging or begging culture in the Seychelles. Food is still so plentiful that mangoes, breadfruit, coconuts, and other fruits go unpicked far longer than elsewhere, and fruit that falls to the ground is often left to rot. On a Sunday afternoon in November the sounds of children sitting in mango trees can be heard echoing through the islands, but, in contrast to a comparable scene in India, many of the children casually throw away fruit that is only half-eaten.

All of this describes a situation in which greater food self-sufficiency could be gained simply by conserving more, making better use of available lands, and eating more domestically produced agricultural products. The thrust of the government's outreach efforts has been to encourage people in precisely these directions, thus far with only a marginal impact. The government's Development Plan for 1980–1984, therefore, seeks to reduce dependence on imported food by enhancing indigenous agricultural capabilities while increasing exports by concentrating on the vast fishing potential of the islands and exploring for oil. Petroleum accounted for 23 percent and manufactured goods for 39 percent of imports in 1979–1980, which, when combined with food (20 percent) and other items (18 percent) produced a total import bill of US$107 million, as compared with total exports of only US$4.6 million. The major items of export are, in descending order of value, copra (US$2.5 million), frozen fish (US$1.4 million), guano (US$0.3 million) and cinnamon bark (US $0.2 million).[9]

AGRICULTURE

Aside from the need to increase food production in order to lessen costly imports and provide for a burgeoning population, government planners are concerned about an accelerating movement of people out of

Figure 4.1. Processing cinnamon for export. Seychelles government photo.

agriculture. Indeed, employment in every sector of the Seychelles economy except agriculture increased in the 1960s and 1970s. Agricultural employment fell by 10 percent between 1971 and 1977, to the point where only 340 of 12,315 households (2.8 percent) earned their primary income from farming.[10] Of these households, 73 are on coconut plantations or large farms – defined as those having more than ten cattle and/or more than fifty pigs – on Mahé or the outlying islands. Most of the remaining farms are 5 acres (2 hectares) or less.

The dominant tradition in Seychelles has been for families – even in urban areas – to maintain small kitchen gardens and a few animals and chickens but to shy away from farming on any larger scale. The 1977 census estimated that more than 40 percent of Seychelles families kept at least one or two pigs in their backyards and more than 50 percent kept chickens. These and other homestead animals and birds are generally allowed to forage for scraps and seeds rather than being fed planned diets, but they are coveted by the population as a means to supplement incomes and are appreciated by the government because they have produced a surprising degree of self-sufficiency in pork and chicken.

The Seychelles government during the British days tried to encourage agriculture by letting out small 5-acre "blocks" of land for nominal rents. However, rules that tenants should work the land and not seek outside employment have not been enforced, resulting in a situation in which most "blockers" simply collect coconuts from the land, pay the small rents, and seek employment in the urban sectors. Most "blockers" and private home owners also have small garden plots and trees where they grow bananas, breadfruit, mangoes, sweet potatoes, and a number of other items for their own use. The present government is seeking to rekindle interest in agriculture through educational and extension programs and by identifying and taking over agricultural lands that are not productive. The rhetoric of both political speeches and a previous development plan spoke of becoming self-sufficient in food by 1982, but, as already indicated, dependence on food imports has in fact been increasing rather than decreasing.

Perhaps the major reason why people are not attracted to agriculture has to do with a lack of income opportunities. A 1978 survey conducted by the government's Statistical Division indicated that the average small farmer earned only US$1,472 per year in total agricultural incomes, from which he had to pay an average of US$592 in production costs.[11] Even if his resulting annual income of US$880 was somewhat underestimated, this low figure goes a long way toward explaining why most small farmers find it necessary to seek supplementary income in the cities (average annual income for all Seychellois households was US $2,957 in 1978). Large farmers also state that their current and capital expenditures exceed their total money income (see Table 4.2), which is the usual explanation for the increasing neglect of the large farms and their unattractiveness to young people from farming families.

Price incentives to farmers are distasteful to the present socialist government, which has instead tried to establish government-run marketing cooperatives for farm products, a national Development Bank that will try to provide easier and more accessible credit to farmers, and a government-owned commodity company (SEYCOM), which seeks to maintain steady prices to the consumer through price controls and will, in the words of President René, eventually "become the sole exporter of all we produce."[12] In January 1979, however, it was found that only 16 of 124 farmers interviewed in a random sample (13 percent) were using the government's marketing cooperatives, the reasoning of the nonusers being (in order of frequency of response) that they could make more profit by selling direct to the public or to private dealers, that payments from the cooperative were not immediate, and that they did not produce enough to warrant use of the cooperative.[13] When asked what government could do to help agriculture, these same farmers focused on development of water resources, reduction of farm input prices, and removal of price controls.

Perhaps because of the yawning gap between the government's en-

TABLE 4.2

Income and Production Costs, Large Farms (Rs.000's per farm)

	Mixed Farms	Livestock Farms	Coconut Farms	All Large Farms
Total income	179.9	427.1	211.4	258.2
Current expenditure	120.1	395.6	118.8	199.9
Capital expenditure	145.1	94.6	91.6	116.6
Total	265.2	490.2	210.4	316.5

Source: Report on the 1978 Agriculture Survey (Victoria: Government Printers, 1980), p. 62.

thusiastic advocacy of a socialist agriculture and the farmer's well-entrenched laissez-faire attitude, every indicator points to a continued migration to the main islands of Mahé and Praslin for employment in tourism and construction, with agriculture increasingly becoming a part-time, ancillary occupation. As both large and small farmers have failed to respond to government programs, government plans for enhanced food production have tended to concentrate on state farms and household plots. Most of the large livestock or fruit and vegetable farms are already owned by the government, including the Union Vale Dairy Farm, the Grand Anse Experimental Farm, and Anse Aux Pins Agricultural Station, all on Mahé. Since 1977 the government has also established four state farms of more than 100 acres (40 hectares) each, growing primarily fruits, vegetables, coffee, and tea.

There is no chance of growing food crops for export on any scale, but there is a possibility that the country might become self-sufficient in at least some foods in the 1980s. Rice is not one of them, as there is not enough land to cultivate rice economically. Agriculturalists have instead encouraged the Seychellois to plant root crops (like yams or cassava) and fruit trees, on small farms or on household plots, with the government guaranteeing one plot for every family as part of its housing program. Small farmers are also being urged to make more effective use of the Seychelles' six to eight months of good weather for growing vegetables.

Some of the most promising government programs are the afforestation and timber projects being developed throughout the country. A large number of rapidly growing Leucaena varieties are being planted, for use as fodder on the more populated islands and in timber lots on the outer islands. Fairly sizable stands of mahogany and other indigenous woods are already well under way. Since 1970, when the construction boom started, Seychelles has been importing (primarily from Malaysia) about 50 percent of its timber requirements, but foresters are now hopeful that new plantings and management techniques will enable the country to become self-sufficient in timber by the year 2000.

Among the least successful agricultural programs have been attempts to maintain sagging coconut production, which fell from 50 million nuts per year in the 1960s to approximately 20 million nuts per year in 1978. The great enemy of Seychelles planters is the *Melittomma*, or stem beetle, which attacks fully grown trees just above the crown of the roots and bores its way around the inside of the trunk. The *Melittomma* has severely affected production of coconuts on some of the granitic islands—including Mahé, Praslin, and Silhouette—although it is not a problem on the coralline islands. Only an expert can detect the *Melittomma*; it must be dug out by hand and the wound coated with creosote if it is not to destroy the tree.

Other sources of damage to coconut trees are rodents that live in the trees and destroy half-grown nuts, trees planted too close together to grow into healthy specimens, lack of adequate water or of proper terracing to preserve water, and insufficient fertilizer. A well-managed estate is one in which trees are planted far apart, hills are terraced, fertilizer is applied at proper intervals and in proper amounts, the *Melittomma* is systematically searched for and dug out of trunks, and fowl are controlled so that they do not eat the tree snakes that feed on rodents. With the increasing costs of labor, fertilizer, and water resources over the last decade, estates have become so expensive to manage that routine tasks are simply not performed. Aside from the *Melittomma*, widespread neglect of such tasks is the major reason for the decline in coconut production.

The government has been reluctant to nationalize the large coconut estates, despite the inequalities they manifest, as the estates are now producing most of the country's exports. Moreover, enormous investments by the government would be necessary if production were to be significantly improved. Attempts are made to provide such things as extension information and new plant varieties, and the government has taken over some plantations that were totally unproductive. A number of agriculturalists have pointed out that steady increases in costs of fertilizer (including guano, the traditional fertilizer, which has become terribly scarce) could be offset by using seaweed, either as a surface manure or (when dried and burned) as a source of potash. Plantation owners argue, however, that the labor costs of using seaweed are still much greater than the expenses involved in transporting guano from the outer islands or importing chemical fertilizers. They also argue that labor and management skills are too expensive to introduce new hybrid coconut varieties and that such varieties are ill suited to the Seychelles in any case. For whatever reason, it is clear that innumerable schemes designed to introduce the hybrids have been unsuccessful.

FISHING

When the René government first came to power, it labeled expansion of the fishing industry its "largest and most important proposal."[14] The value of exports of frozen fish grew to US$1.4 million a year by 1981, but this is a drop in the bucket when compared to the expectations that most Seychellois have for the future. Moreover, most of today's exports come from the catches of small family fishermen going out in little boats for a few hours each day or landing fish on beaches; such fishermen bring in an estimated 4,000 tons of fish (mainly carangue, bonito, mackerel, cordonnier, and becune) each year.[15] What the Seychelles government would now like to develop is large-scale commercial fishing, concentrating first on tuna and later on a number of other fish (including prawns, lobster, barracuda, marlin, bonito, wahoo, tunny, kingfish, and sailfish).

Fish have always been the major source of protein for the Seychelles, but most of the fishing has been done from boats close into shore or from beach seines or cassiers (fish traps). There is such a wealth of fish in Seychelles waters that these methods have always been more than sufficient for home consumption; indeed, many fishermen still bury much of their catch during bountiful periods when the sea is calm. The availability and price of fish does fluctuate considerably, depending essentially on weather conditions, but the present government is hoping to flatten out price variations by selling through SEYCOM frozen fish as an alternative to fresh fish. The 1977 census estimated that 420 households own a boat used primarily for fishing and 842 households either own or "part-own" fishing gear.[16] These figures indicate that fishing, like agriculture, is spread out among a number of small-scale household producers, with many of them pursuing fishing only as a supplementary source of income. On the whole, however, fishing has tended to be more lucrative than small-scale agriculture.

The government expects the fishing sector to be "the most important source of new employment over the next few years."[17] To develop large-scale commercial fishing, a state company called SNAFIC (the Seychelles National Fishing Company) has been formed, but nationalization is not considered feasible for the small-scale demersal (beach fishing) industry. What the government is trying to do is to provide assistance to small fishermen for building or purchasing boats at the

Figure 4.2. Seychellois fishermen going out in the morning. There are literally hundreds of small family-sized boats of this type on the islands. Photo courtesy *Nation.*

same time constructing cold stores, a cannery, and blast freezers as processing and marketing facilities. Some idea of the extent to which fishing projects have failed to meet expectations in recent years can be gained by contrasting the goal of 4,000 tons of tuna per annum anticipated in the 1980–1984 Development Plan with the total of only 215 tons actually landed in 1980.[18]

Large-scale commercial fishing never developed in the Seychelles after a big Colonial Development Corporation scheme failed dismally in 1951 and the British concluded that development of a fishing industry in the islands was a losing proposition.[19] The British themselves never did much fishing in the Indian Ocean, as they had more and better-established rights and far greater experience in the Atlantic. The largest exclusive rights in the Western Indian Ocean are, perhaps surprisingly, those of the French, who still own outright dozens of small islands, including the Kerguelen and Crozet groups as well as New Amsterdam, St. Paul, Tromelin, Réunion, and numerous others. Many of the French islands are uninhabited; some are only occasionally visited by French explorers or scientists monitoring meteorological or other technical equip-

Figure 4.3. Seychellois fishermen with their catch. Photo courtesy *Nation*.

Figure 4.4. A fish-seller at New Market, Victoria. Author's photo.

ment. The fact that they are French possessions gives France the ex-clusive economic rights to the seas around them.

The Seychelles has the second largest exclusive economic zone in the Western Indian Ocean, and it has established a 200-mile (320-kilometer) exclusive limit beyond and adjacent to its 12-mile (19-kilometer) territorial waters (see Figure 1.1). It does license foreign vessels to fish in its waters, for a substantial fee, and it tries to enforce practices that promote conservation and protect the ecology of the area. Two of the major problems confronting the Seychelles government are how to patrol its waters to protect its fishing and other economic rights and how to develop an expertise in deep-sea fishing. To cope with the first problem the government has acquired one oceangoing vessel and two interisland craft to patrol the outer islands, which are often more than 600 miles (960 kilometers) distant from Victoria. These are in addition to smaller aircraft and police launches that carry out patrols in the vicinity of Mahé. Government negotiations with both the French and Indian navies about the possibility of using their existing manpower to assist in catching poachers has thus far yielded no results. Some Seychellois have been so concerned about the illegal fishing being done by South Korea and Japan that they have suggested an approach to the United States to see if U.S. satellites might be available to track down errant boats of other nations.

Since independence, several South Korean ships have been found shipwrecked on various Seychelles islands, some of them carrying loads of tuna. Because the Koreans claimed that they had caught the fish outside Seychelles waters, the government simply treated the vessels as "neutral ships run aground," providing hospitality for their survivors while facilitating transportation home.[20] Privately, however, everyone in the Seychelles was convinced that the South Koreans, and to a larger extent the Japanese, were illegally fishing Seychelles waters on a massive scale. Therefore, when a Japanese fishing vessel, the *Sumi Maru* (Figure 4.5) was caught in the act of fishing illegally by a Seychelles patrol in 1980, the Seychelles government seized the ship and confiscated it along with its catch. Both a Seychelles court and the International Court of Justice at The Hague ruled that the Japanese had to pay a heavy fine to the Seychelles government, and both agreed that Seychelles could legally retain possession of the Japanese fishing vessel.[21]

The difficulty for the Seychellois is that they do not know how to operate the Japanese vessel, and, of course, the Japanese are not about to teach them. Moreover, relationships with South Korea have deteriorated, in part because of fishing disputes, in part because of conflicting ideologies. Seychelles is negotiating with the North Koreans to see if they can teach Seychellois how to use the very sophisticated ship that has been "acquired" from Japan. But thus far, only the Japanese, South Koreans, and Taiwanese have developed the art of "long-line" fishing, which is the method used by the *Sumi Maru*.

The major large-scale fishing project that Seychelles has undertaken involved four tuna clippers that were delivered from France in 1980, two of them coming as part of an aid package and two of them on soft loans. In preparation for the anticipated catch from these ships, the Seychelles government sought and obtained from the British substantial aid for the construction of a new fishing harbor and cold storage

Figure 4.5. The *Sumi Maru No. 25*, fishing trawler seized from Japan and confiscated by the Seychelles when it was caught fishing illegally in Seychelles
waters. Author's photo.

facilities. Unfortunately, these four tuna clippers turned out to be inap-
propriate to the needs of Seychelles. Seychelles fishermen claimed that
they sailed too high off the water to enable the catch to be readily pulled
in. French diplomats have suggested that both they and the Seychelles
government went into the tuna fishing scheme with inadequate knowledge and too little patience. A prominent reason for the collapse of the
scheme was that both sides discovered too late that the live bait they
needed for the method of fishing they had chosen was at an impractical
and uneconomical distance from the waters where they proposed to fish.

     Both sides now admit that the Franco-Seychelles fishing scheme
was launched with insufficient prior research and experimentation.
Despite their vast holdings in the Indian Ocean, the French have always
concentrated their overseas fishing efforts on the west coast of Africa
and they have traditionally pursued a method of deepsea fishing that involves an intricate use of purse nets. For the Seychelles project, both the
French and Seychelles governments decided to use a "pole and line"
method that is far more labor-intensive than either the use of nets or the
long-line method perfected by the Japanese. This choice was preferred
by the Seychellois because it would provide greater employment
possibilities. French diplomats now claim that Seychellois fishermen
were either not strong enough or they were unwilling to make the exer-

Figure 4.6. The *Aldabra,* one of four ships provided to the Seychelles by the French and then taken back. The Seychellois complained that the ships sailed too high off the water to be effective in the "pole and line" method of fishing. Photo courtesy *Nation.*

tion necessary to use the "pole and line" method, thus producing complaints that the ships were constructed too high off the water. The pole and line method has been used successfully with similar ships in the Basque country (bordering on France and Spain), and it is also being pursued with success in Southeast Asia. The French cite as proof of the technical acceptability of the ships they supplied the fact that all four were sold to New Caledonia shortly after the Seychelles government asked the French government to take them back in January 1981.

Despite the failure of the original Franco-Seychelles fishing scheme, in the early 1980s both governments were still exploring possible collaboration for the future. The French are interested in such collaboration because they want to develop as much expertise and skill as possible in order to exploit their resources elsewhere in the Indian Ocean. Seychelles has also concluded cooperative fishing agreements with the Spanish and the Germans, who will explore use of the pole and line and purse net methods of fishing respectively. Other alternatives for Seychelles would be the British or the Americans who have less interest in fishing in the Indian Ocean, or the Russians. As explained elsewhere, the determination of Seychelles to remain nonaligned has been a major consideration in sticking it out with the French despite failures.

Negotiations are under way with a number of countries for fishing vessels equipped with refrigeration facilities, blast freezers, fish processing plants, and other equipment. The government is constructing a cannery, with hopes that large amounts of fish will eventually be canned for export. Already built are cold storage facilities in most districts of Mahé, where fish can be deep-frozen and ice produced. As Maxime Fayon has pointed out, the availability of ice has enabled small fishermen to go to more distant fishing grounds and to stay longer at sea.[22]

MANPOWER DEVELOPMENT

Whether it be fishing, agriculture, tourism, or any other economic activity they want to pursue, the biggest obstacle for the Seychellois has always been acquisition of high-quality skills and the technical competence among enough people to assure the viability of a new enterprise. In a nation of only 65,000 people, so isolated that its nearest neighbor is a thousand miles or more distant, either expatriates with required skills must be brought in to teach locals or locals must be sent abroad for training. Throughout the 1970s there were always at least a thousand expatriates in Seychelles, providing training and consultancies or technical skills—primarily in tourism and construction but in other fields as well—and almost a thousand Seychellois went abroad for training or work each year.[23] There is no question that the better educated and better trained have increasingly formed the elite segments of the Seychelles population.

Among those sent abroad for training, most tend to return to Seychelles. Their return is encouraged by a "bonding" system that requires nonreturnees to forfeit large deposits made to the government at the time of departure. A recent survey of 172 students trained in the United Kingdom between 1977 and 1979, for example, showed that only 8 percent of those surveyed failed to return to Seychelles after completing their studies.[24] Unfortunately, no data exist on the occupational characteristics of permanent leavers, who generally go abroad for employment rather than study; according to the most reliable estimates, Seychelles loses approximately a hundred and fifty workers per year, with one-third of them being considered skilled workers.[25] Economists who use such figures to describe a "brain drain" suggest that most of the skilled laborers who permanently leave the Seychelles are employed abroad in precisely those jobs (including medicine and accountancy) for which large numbers of expatriates are hired in Seychelles.[26]

The present government is not isolationist, but it is socialist and egalitarian. Although it continues to hire expatriates and to send Seychellois abroad for advanced training, it has set as a standard of its success a goal of equalizing incomes among the various strata of the population. At the same time, the government now provides a much wider variety of indigenous educational and vocational opportunities for those in the lower income groups. President René has explained his socialist convictions as an outgrowth of the argument that Seychelles is a place where "the wealth of our society and, therefore, the means for each of us to achieve a better life depends on the quality of our labour."[27] René went on to argue that the only way to achieve more productivity of labor is through greater equality and socialism. "A man who does not work," René says, "is an exploiter." In Seychelles, he argues, "we cannot afford to have members who merely consume and do not produce."

Although there is considerable support for many aspects of the new socialist programs that have been introduced, there is enormous controversy surrounding almost every one of them. By far the most controversial policy has been the complete restructuring of the educational system, including the establishment of the highly politicized National Youth Service (NYS). The old elite private primary and secondary school for girls—Regina Mundi Convent School—has been abolished; the old elite private primary and secondary school for boys (Seychelles College, previously run by Canadian priests but taken over by the government) is scheduled to go out of existence in 1984. Primary education has been restructured so that exams that previously forced some children to drop out of school after grade six are now given after grade nine; education for eleven years is now free for all Seychelles citizens. At the end of grade nine—at age 16 or so—every student is encouraged to join the National Youth Service for two years. For the present the NYS is voluntary; a little more than half of those eligible for it (850 of 1,500 or so) have joined. By 1984, when Seychelles College is to be abolished, there will be no alternative school available on the islands for 16- and 17- year-olds. Further pressure to join the NYS stems from a 1981 law that forbids employment to anyone under 18 years of age. The combination of the 1981 law and the 1984 abolition of Seychelles College will create a situation in which a Seychelles 16-year-old will have to go abroad for further education beyond the ninth grade, join the NYS, or sit at home idle.

The NYS campus is located on the scenic but rough-hewn northwest coast of Mahé, at Port Launnay. Students study traditional courses like mathematics, French, and English, but the emphasis is on practical vocational subjects like agriculture, fishing, carpentry, and so forth, all of which are taught by resident craftsmen called *animateurs*. This kind of education will enable some students to pass the British O (ordinary)-

Figure 4.7. The opening of the National Youth Service on the beach at Port Launnay. Photo courtesy Seychelles Agence Press.

level exams, intended for those who do not wish to go on to the university. According to present plans, the NYS will not offer the A (advanced)-level exams, designed for the university-bound. Seychellois students can presently prepare for the A-level exams at Seychelles College in lieu of joining the NYS. When the college is abolished, university-bound students will be required to spend two years in the NYS before they can prepare for the A-level exams at a newly-created National Pedagogical Institute. Most students, however, will be expected to go on from the NYS to one or two years of study at the Teachers Training Institute, the Hotel Catering School, Nursing School, a newly created Polytechnic, or into other technical schools or programs located on the islands.

When the NYS was first broached in 1979 it was to be compulsory for everyone from age 15, but there were two days (11 and 12 October) of massive and violent student rioting against it by almost three thousand students—in a country which had never previously witnessed a single student riot.[28] The president then backed down and settled on the present plan, which is voluntary until 1984 and starts at age 16. Since 1979, more and more elite Seychelles families have sent their children abroad for schooling and a number of families have permanently moved to Europe, Australia, or elsewhere for the sake of the education of their

children. Evaluations of the first year of operation of the NYS have confirmed what was already widely known beforehand, that the brightest
students are seldom challenged academically. At the same time, the
quality of education at Seychelles College has deteriorated, in part
because its funds have dried up but largely because its superb faculty
either has been dispersed throughout the rest of the school system by the
government or has left the Seychelles.

Aside from the emphasis on work-study and vocational (as opposed
to academic) training, many parents and students object to the NYS
because it requires that every student spend two years at the NYS campus *without spending a single night at home for the entire two years*. Students
are allowed to visit their parents for two twelve-hour periods a month,
on alternate Sundays from 6 A.M. to 6 P.M.; parents are permitted to visit
the NYS campus on appointed days at intervals of several months.
Students are not allowed to take vacations from NYS for a period of more
than twelve hours during the entire two-year period. Many parents and
students also object to the kind of political education that is required of
all students at the NYS campus, which consists in large measure of
discussions designed to convince students of the wisdom of the
Seychelles People's Progressive Front (SPPF) brand of socialism, taught
by party members and *animateurs* trained in the social sciences. Military
training "as such" is not given by the NYS, but, in the words of President
René, students are "involved in learning the basic principles of drill and
parade as well as the development of a high degree of vigilance."[29]
Florence Benstrong, coordinator of the NYS, has stated flatly that any
student who fundamentally disagrees with the SPPF program or who ex-
presses displeasure with President René "does not belong" on the NYS
campus. Such a student, she said, "would be sent home."[30]

Benstrong, a former primary school headmistress, argued that the
NYS provides students with practical experience in life, as all of them
must do their own laundry, cook their own meals, maintain and repair
their own dormitories, and make many of their own rules in group sessions and self-governing committees. At the same time, she said,
students learn discipline because they are expected to be at morning ex-
ercise sessions at 6 A.M., are regularly inspected for cleanliness, are required to be at classes and meals on time, and must participate in farming, fishing, animal husbandry, construction projects, and trips to the
outer islands.

Girls and boys live separately at NYS, in dormitory situations
called clusters, but they work and study and socialize together.
Benstrong admitted that the brighter students—and especially those in
the basic sciences—are not being challenged academically, but suggested
that such students are compensated by the invaluable experiences of

Figure 4.8. Students during morning drills at the National Youth Service campus on Port Launnay. Seychelles government photo.

work-study. Neither the sciences nor history is taught as a separate subject; they are instead integrated into month-long practicums (for example, biology is studied as part of a practicum on agriculture or animal husbandry; physics is pursued during practicums on construction or technology; history is taught in the practicum called culture, which also includes political education). The real value of the NYS, in Benstrong's view, is for the poorer students, who often view the NYS as an alternative to homes where drunkenness, child-beating, and illegitimate children are the rule rather than the exception. For such students, two straight years on the beach campus at Port Launnay without a night at home is often a blessing rather than a curse.

From the perspective of the government, the real pay-off from the NYS is expected to be the creation of a new kind of teenager, who will presumably have more practical skills than those possessed by present-day teenagers, plus a degree of discipline that the government has concluded cannot be fostered in most Seychellois homes. Some social workers are hoping that the presence of teenage girls on the NYS campus from ages 16–18 will diminish the numbers of illegitimate children born to teenagers, as sexual intercourse is forbidden among students—although experiences during the first year have indicated that many girls had to be expelled from the NYS because they had violated all rules and became pregnant. Similarly, the NYS is designed to eliminate drunkenness among teenagers: Liquor is prohibited on the campus, students are not allowed to visit hotels, and the only legitimate bar outside the hotels is located on the other side of Mahé and is not allowed to serve people under 18. Nevertheless, several students have been dropped from the NYS for drunkenness, and some students and *animateurs* admit that students spend a great deal of time establishing supply lines of liquor from sources outside the campus.

Government officials have suggested that they might not be able to diminish the incidence of illegitimacy and drunkenness among this generation of teenagers, but they are convinced that they can do it with future generations. A major study by the Seychelles Year of the Child Commission, in which President René's wife Geva played a major role, has concluded that the basic ills of Seychelles society stem from poverty and a breakdown of the family. According to this study, more than half (56 percent) of all children ages 1–4 are undernourished and 32 percent of all children ages 14 and over have dropped out of school.[31] To provide healthy alternatives to a badly eroded family life, the government has established compulsory day care centers for all children 4–7 years old and is in the process of setting up voluntary day care centers for children between the ages of 1 and 4. The health needs of children are supposed to be better met by the new nationalized health service and by a school lunch program that provides every child in school with a free lunch. Many special programs have been established for the handicapped.

Housing standards, which are often poor—only 48 percent of all homes have a water tap, only 33 percent have a toilet, 26 percent of the population lives in one- or two-room homes that have more than three people per room—are to be improved by a government housing program in which house-sites and loans for building are provided. Some idea of the magnitude of the task facing the government can be gained from the recent National Development Plan, in which the government estimated that 3,000 new homes would have to be constructed during the five-year period 1980–1984 to satisfy present and projected needs. As compared with these needs, total government housing loans during the three-year period 1977–1980 numbered only 812, and most of these loans were for the improvement and maintenance of existing homes rather than the building of new ones. A full employment scheme operates in such a way that anyone can secure work between the hours of 7 and 12 on a normal working day, being paid Rs.20 (US$3.20) for five hours of labor.[32] As most of the work available consists of collecting garbage, cleaning foul drains, or removing refuse heaps, the full employment scheme has not been heavily subscribed. Current estimates are that 300 people are using the scheme regularly, while the numbers of unemployed seeking work were listed in the 1977 census at more than 2,600.

SOCIALISM AND ITS CRITICS

The most ardent opponents of the SPPF have left the country, but a good many people in leadership positions have serious doubts about the efficacy of at least some aspects of the new regime. Opponents are, understandably, not vocal about their dissent, but there is, nonetheless, considerable grousing in private. President René has argued that his government has instituted so many socialist programs, affecting so many areas of life, that it would be impossible now for any successor government to go back on his socialist commitment. At least one of his leading advisers, however, was willing to venture a personal evaluation that "most of the new programs are not working," leading this adviser to express a hunch that "our socialism will not last ten years."

The private criticisms that one hears most frequently are as follows:

1. Radical actions have been taken quickly, without sufficient planning or prior study. This has produced severe discontinuities, widespread apprehension among the populace, and inferior programs.
2. The only citizens closely consulted about changes have been the most active party members, who account for a tiny and unrepresentative segment of the population.
3. The government has abolished the two best schools in the Seychelles and has replaced them with an educational system that severely disadvantages the brighter students interested in academic pursuits.
4. Many of the best people in the Seychelles, with leadership and technical skills, have been forced to move abroad, including many teachers, doctors, journalists, businessmen, and investors.
5. The highest levels of technology and many future leaders among the youth have been neglected, so that A-level students, for example, will be disadvantaged when competing with students in Europe or Australia, the two areas where most Seychellois go to college.
6. Political ideology has been introduced into the educational system unnecessarily.
7. Both the National Health Service and the educational system will inevitably deteriorate as a result of too rapid an expansion

and excessive bureaucratization since 1977. Seychellois doctors are being encouraged to set up private practices in foreign countries because they cannot have private practices in the Seychelles.

8. Businessmen have been severely affected by government price controls, severe cutbacks in foreign investment, a general slowdown of the economy, the decline in tourism, and government takeovers of businesses and business functions.

Some of the most severe public criticism of the government has come from the nation's doctors, who met together before the nationalization of the health service in 1979 and submitted a memorandum in which they unanimously advocated an alternative to the government program and pleaded that more thought and study be given to the consequences of change before a drastic revision of the existing system was undertaken.[33] Many doctors and other leaders in society argue that the way to tackle problems like overpopulation and illegitimacy is not through socialist programs, but rather through taking on the Catholic church. The church continues to be powerful enough to prevent a liberal abortion law, restrict use of contraceptives to only one-third of the women in reproductive age groups, and limit divorces to less than a dozen a year, all the while sanctioning en ménage arrangements by baptizing illegitimate children in the church only on condition that the names of the mother and father are known. These same critics suggest that the way to diminish the incidence of poverty is to boost economic production, which can be done only with a greater turnover of tourists, more effective development of the fishing industry, more incentives to farmers, and attraction of foreign investment.

The government seldom responds to such criticism in public, but officials will argue in private that they need even greater powers, more state-run institutions, and more time for things to start working. In the meantime, government involvement in the economy continues to expand. Among the many government corporations and parastatals that have been set up since 1977, in addition to those already mentioned, are the Seychelles National Commodity Company, Seychelles Timber Company, Aviation Seychelles, Air Seychelles, Seychelles Agricultural Development Company (SADECO), Islands Development Company, (IDC), National Fruit Nursery, State Assurance Company, Compagnie Seychelloise Pour La Promotion Hotelière (COSPROH), Seychelles National Investment Corporation (SNIC), Development Bank of Seychelles, the Seychelles Monetary Authority, and a number of smaller enterprises that are either being planned or already operating. These include industries for processing copra into coconut oil, a pig farm for processed pork products, a salt production works, a hydroponic farm, a fruit juice and milk-processing factory, a hotel to be constructed in the Victoria town center, a tourist hotel in the exquisite Beau Vallon area, a sawmill, an air catering service, a bottling plant, cinnamon production units, and units for using fish heads to produce silage and fish meal—all government-owned. In addition, the government is hoping to "reorganize" the tea and dairy industries and has threatened to take over the tourist industry.[34]

Government leaders are quick to point out that they do not have a policy of "general nationalization of private enterprise," although they are willing to buy up land, hotels, and businesses when they become unviable or run into financial difficulties, or when "for public purposes it is deemed necessary."[35] Private investors, of course, worry that the government might itself enact measures to make a business unviable and then buy it at a cheap price without calling the action "nationalization." Officially, the government is encouraging foreign investment in hotels on Praslin (but not on Mahé or any of the other islands) and would like more foreign investors in export industries. Negotiations are also under way to entice some of the major oil companies to explore Seychelles waters, but those that have been approached are reportedly reluctant to become heavily involved since AMOCO pulled out in early 1981 after drilling for more than five years.

Government bankers argue that they have an attractive investment climate for the "serious foreign investor," as foreign firms are free to repatriate any amount of after-tax profits and are generally exempted from import duties for the first few years of operation. But taxes are high (35 percent on profits and 35 percent on personal incomes plus 10 percent of the total wage bill and 5 percent of personal incomes for social security), and in addition to taxes, all expatriates working in the Seychelles must pay an annual fee of Rs.10,000 (US$1,600) for a work permit. Under the circumstances, foreign investors have not been coming into the Seychelles since the 1977 coup, with the exception of a few joint ventures in which a foreign company holds minority shares and/or a service contract. Ironically enough, most of the parastatals and newly created government enterprises are being run by expatriates; in some cases expatriate-run government enterprises have replaced businesses that were previously run by Seychellois.

President René and the SPPF are convinced that they have majority support among the population for their socialist programs, but they are unwilling to test that conviction in competitive party elections. They reason that such benefits as free medical care, free education, and a Rs.300 (US$48) per month pension for more than four thousand retirees are enough to instill in large segments of the population "gratitude for the efforts which the [SPPF] has made."[36] The insecurity of the government, however, is indicated by its continued repression of all opposition and by the general tone of its approach to dissent. That tone was exhibited by President René in the same speech in which he identified "gratitude" among the vast bulk of the population, when he asked and answered questions about dissent as follows:

> Why is it, therefore, that some people still refuse to acknowledge reality? Why is it that some still try to impede our progress? Why is it that some still refuse to play their part to create a better and more prosperous society? Why is it that some still continue to live a life of laziness and drunkenness? Why is it that some continue to encourage disorder in our country? Why is it that some continue to be more jealous than Cain?
>
> There are some good-for-nothings, some parasites in our society, who treat those who work as bootlickers and suckers. These people, whose hearts are burning with jealousy, are well known to us. I can only give them a small piece of advice—"try to emulate these bootlickers."[37]

NOTES

1. F. D. Ommanney, *Shoals of Capricorn* (London: Longmans Green and Company, 1952), pp. 136–137.

2. Douglas Alexander, *Holiday in Seychelles: A Guide to the Islands* (Capetown: Purnell Publishers, 1972), p. 86.

3. These figures are taken from Republic of Seychelles, *National Development Plan, 1978–1982* (Victoria: Government Printers, 1978). Other excellent sources of economic data are (1) *Seychelles: Economic Memorandum* (Washington: Eastern Africa Regional Office, World Bank, 1980); and (2) *Employment and Poverty in the Seychelles: Report of a Study Organised by the Institute of Development Studies*, Percy Selwyn, Chairman (Brighton: University of Sussex, 1980). The first of these is a World Bank country study prepared by Robert Maubouche and Naimeh Hadjitarkhani; the second is a two-volume report prepared by a team of seven scholars.

4. E. Faure, "Seychelles Economy: Its Problems and Prospects," in *Recherche et réflexion sur la société seychellois: Une définition des problèmes sociaux* [Research and reflection on Seychellois society: A definition of social problems] (Victoria: Ministry of Labour and Social Services, 1980), p. 49.

5. *Nation*, June 25, 1981, p. 2.

6. France Albert René, *Budget Address, 1981* (Victoria: Government Printers, 1981), p. 1.

7. Burton Benedict, *People of the Seychelles*, 3rd ed., Ministry of Overseas Development, Overseas Research Publication No. 14 (London: Her Majesty's Stationery Office, 1970), pp. 42ff.

8. Republic of Seychelles, *Statistical Bulletin, Fourth Quarter, 1980*, Vol. 1.,

no. 3 (Victoria: Government Printers, 1981), p. 16.

9. Ibid., p. 17.

10. *National Development Plan, 1978-1982*, p. 27. See also Republic of Seychelles, *1977 Census Report* (Victoria: Government Printers, 1978), pp. 123ff.

11. Figures are from Republic of Seychelles, *Report on the 1978 Agriculture Survey* (Victoria: Government Printers, March 1980), pp. 65ff. All Seychelles figures are from Republic of Seychelles, *Report on the 1978 Household Expenditure Survey* (Victoria: Government Printers, 1979), p. 64.

12. René, *Budget Address, 1981*, p. 4.

13. *1978 Agriculture Survey*, pp. 70-71.

14. *National Development Plan, 1978-1982*, p. 37.

15. *Statistical Bulletin, Fourth Quarter, 1980*, p. 24.

16. *1977 Census Report*, p. 130.

17. *National Development Plan, 1980-1984* (Victoria: Government Printers, 1980), p. 26.

18. Compare ibid. with *Statistical Bulletin, Fourth Quarter, 1980*, p. 24.

19. C. Ratcliffe, "Offshore Fishing in the Seychelles," *Oceanology International, 1975* (London), pp. 141-151.

20. The incidents are detailed in *Lettre des Seychelles* (monthly review), August 1978, p. 4.

21. See *Nation*, Vol. 5, no. 12 (January 17 and 20, 1981), p. 1.

22. Maxime Fayon, *Geography of Seychelles*, 2nd rev. ed. (Victoria: Ministry of Education and Culture, 1978), p. 30.

23. *Statistical Bulletin, Fourth Quarter, 1980*, p. 21.

24. *Seychelles Manpower Review, 1979* (Victoria: Government Printing Office, January 1980), Appendix 2.

25. This is the estimate of the Sussex University team that visited the Seychelles in 1979-1980. See *Employment and Poverty in The Seychelles*, Vol. 1, p. 50.

26. See, for example, "Training Overseas: A Survey of Seychellois Undergoing Training Overseas," Ministry of Labour and Social Service, October 1979 (mimeo), p. 16.

27. All quotes in this paragraph are from René, *Budget Address, 1981*, p. 2.

28. The riots are described in some detail in the last issue of *Weekend Life*, Vol. 3, no. 16 (October 27, 1979), pp. 4-5. After publication of this issue, *Weekend Life* was closed by the government, and its editor and publisher, Bernard Verlaque, was eventually arrested and forced into exile. He and his wife are presently living and working in Nairobi.

29. France Albert René, *The Seychelles National Youth Service: What It Aims to Do and How It Will Be Run* (Victoria: Ministry of Education and Information, 1980), pp. 8-9.

30. This and subsequent quotations come from author's interview, June 1981.

31. Figures are from *Nou Bane Zanfans: A Report and Working Paper for the Seychelles International Year of the Child Commission* (Victoria: Government Printers, 1980), pp. 4-5, 17ff.

32. See W.P.B. Noad, "The Full Employment Scheme," in *Recherche et réflexion*, p. 66.

33. *Weekend Life*, Vol. 1, no. 48 (May 27, 1978), p. 3.

34. *National Development Plan, 1980–1984*, p. 16.

35. Ibid., p. 17.

36. *The People*, June 5, 1981, p. 8.

37. Ibid.

5

Change

Among all the changes that have taken place in Seychelles in the 1970s and 1980s, the most salient to the Seychellois themselves have been alterations in the ecology of the islands and the country's dramatic entry into relationships with the rest of the world. Change has taken place on such a scale in these two spheres that many Seychellois express a feeling of nostalgia, or at least a wish for a respite from what they see as a total break with the past. Some of the romantic and poetic aspects of Seychellois life remain, but increasingly the potential commercial and strategic importance of the islands intrudes, bringing in its wake unprecedented strains and tensions.

TOURISM AND ECOLOGY

A major concern of Seychellois leaders has been to promote tourism without damaging the natural beauty and wildlife treasures of the islands. This is a particularly important issue, as many Seychellois do feel that tourism is "not dignified," that the youth of the country are being reduced to "a new class of servitors, barmen and waitresses," or that the Seychellois have "lost some of their best beaches."[1] One of the most attractive features of the new hotels that are being built is the way in which they do use indigenous materials like granite, palm leaves, coral, and native woods (takamaka, casuarina, mango, bamboo, sangdragon, albezia, kapok, breadfruit, bois de nappe, mahogany, calice du pape, and many other woods are available on the islands). The hotels are also generally pleasing in appearance because they are required by law to be lower than the surrounding coconut palms and other vegetation.

Some of the islands have come under the complete protection of international societies after successful international campaigns in the 1960s to preserve the plant life, sea life, shell life, and animals. Aldabra, which at one time had almost been given over to the United States as a naval base, was the object of a massive Save Aldabra campaign—led by the Royal Society of Britain, the Smithsonian Institution, and the U.S.

National Academy of Sciences – that attracted worldwide attention.[2] In the mid-nineteenth century, Charles Darwin and his friends had appealed to the Royal Society to preserve Aldabra in the interests of science, there being no other place in the world so unaffected by human contact where rare studies of evolution and biological processes could be undertaken. The Save Aldabra campaign of the 1960s was bolstered by Darwin's writings on the subject and by support from people like Jacques Cousteau – who had wanted to turn Aldabra into a zoological museum from the time when he first visited the island in 1954 – and world-renowned biologists like Dr. David Stoddart of Cambridge University.[3]

Aldabra now has only nine human residents, these being administrators and staff of the Royal Society who are maintaining the island as a sanctuary for rare species of animals and birds, like the Galapagos-type tortoise (there are more than 100,000 of them on Aldabra, many weighing up to 500 pounds (225 kilograms) each and some of them more than two hundred years old), frigate birds with 7-foot (210-centimeter) wingspans, and the white-throated rail, the only flightless bird surviving in the Western Indian Ocean. Similarly, Desnoeufs and Bird islands are the breeding grounds of colonies of terns and noddies numbering in the millions. Cousin Island was given over to the International Council for Bird Preservation in 1968 and is now administered by two representatives of the society, the only humans allowed to live on the island.[4]

The Seychelles can quickly stir the emotions of anyone interested in conservation and the environment. Sixteen forms of land birds are unique to the Seychelles, including the Seychelles kestrel (the world's smallest falcon), the Seychelles black parrot, the paradise flycatcher, the scops white-eyed owl, the magpie robin, the noddy tern, the redheaded turtle dove, and the brush warbler.[5] In addition, eighty species of plant life are found only in the Seychelles, including the Coco-de-Mer or "double coconut." One species of plant unique to the Seychelles – the Medusagyne or jellyfish plant – was believed extinct until 1971 when it was rediscovered.[6]

The Coco-de-Mer is such a legendary plant that it has been the subject of many books all by itself.[7] The female seed of the Coco-de-Mer bears a remarkable resemblance to the human female pelvis, complete with pubic hair; the male catkin of the Coco-de-Mer is very phallic. One of the myths of the islands is that the Coco-de-Mer reproduces only at night and in the same manner as the human being, but that anyone who witnesses the act of mating is instantly transformed into a Coco-de-Mer. General Charles ("Chinese") Gordon of Khartoum, who visited the Seychelles for several months in 1881, wrote a small manuscript in

Figure 5.1. Sooty terns on Bird Island. Seychelles government photo.

which he described the Seychelles as the orginal Garden of Eden and the Coco-de-Mer as Adam and Eve's Tree of Knowledge.[8] Indian and Javanese rajahs and nizams—and later some European princes and Chinese emperors—have coveted the Coco-de-Mer as an aphrodisiac and have paid extraordinary prices for a single nut. Julian Mockford has described the ways in which the Coco-de-Mer has been used as a sexually stimulating elixir:

> After the thick husk has been cut away, the large twin nut is cracked open. There, in each of the two sections, is found an oval jelly jacketed with thin peel. The jelly is transparent and either faint pink or cloudy white, like the white of a moonstone. As a sweet after dinner the jelly is excellent, and it is in this way that the islanders take it. . . . But in the East, the potent jelly is distributed sparingly, in special concoctions made according to the secret rites of esoteric societies. Whatever the effect of that medicine, which is equally sought after by the Indians and Chinese who come under the spell of its dispensers, there is no doubt about one thing: the islanders swear by the jelly as an immediate rejuvenator.[9]

Current conservation policy is largely the result of a 1970 report by John Proctor, a leading conservation adviser to the British government.[10] Proctor recommended a strategy of controls (prohibitions, closed seasons, and so forth) and the establishment of the National Park and Nature Conservancy Commission to oversee special reserves where wildlife protection would take precedence over all other matters. Specific measures—such as banning the catapult on La Digue Island, placing a bounty on the barn owl, imposing formidable fines and punishment for collection of the triton shell, and outlawing use of fishing spears or harpoons—have been in effect since 1963.[11] Efforts have also been made since the opening of the airport in 1971 to prevent the spread of human and animal diseases by strict enforcement of international travel regulations (planes are routinely sprayed ten minutes before landing, inoculations are rigorously checked, and an island has been set aside for use as a quarantine station).[12]

Despite all these precautions, it is clear that increasing contact between the Seychelles and the outside world is taking its toll. John Jourdain, the first European explorer to record a visit to the Seychelles (in 1609), found the islands densely covered by trees and other plant life that had evolved over millions of years, resulting in forest carpets of rich black humus and guano.[13] The only mammals he noticed on the islands were a few species of fruit bats (also called flying foxes). He complained of a large number of alligators. Today there are no alligators left on any of the islands, most of the guano has been mined and exported, and much of the forest cover has been removed. The first settlers, who came in the 1770s, set a pattern of economic activity that has persisted until the present and that has unquestionably been disastrous for much of the natural wealth that had attracted Jourdain. Rather than settle down to a nonexploitative domesticated agriculture, the first settlers chose to live primarily off the tortoise and seabird population and the coconut palms, exporting timber in exchange for whatever nonindigenous clothing, food, or other items they might need.

The pattern of life set by the early settlers has continued and has been reinforced over the last two hundred years. Hundreds of thousands of turtles were exported from the Seychelles during this period, until export of most turtle species was completely banned in 1968. Green turtles have been especially vulnerable to hunting by man because the female green turtle lays six batches of up to 200 eggs per batch during a three-month period at predictable times every three years. During the laying season, female green turtles will lie offshore without moving very far and will make regular visits to the beach at intervals of about two weeks to lay their eggs. If a female is captured before her first visit to the beach during one of these laying periods, it means the killing of 1,200 eggs in that season. Since 1925 it has been illegal to kill female turtles as they wait offshore, but full protection of females was not provided until 1962, when a closed season was declared. Even now, some violation of turtling laws takes place, simply because it is physically impossible to fully enforce such laws.[14]

A similar situation exists for seabird eggs, which are consumed in enormous quantities by the Seychellois and were at one time exported to Mauritius and other islands. Until 1933 there were no restrictions on the cropping of eggs, but the British then introduced a closed season. After World War II more restrictions were introduced and the export of eggs was banned. The Seychellois still consume more than a million seabird eggs a year, the greatest delicacy being those of the sooty tern, even though all the main bird islands are rigorously patrolled. Some idea of the effect of large-scale seabird egg cropping over the past centuries can be gained from recent estimates that there were fewer than a quarter million sooty terns on Desnoeufs Island in 1970, compared with 5 million in 1931.[15]

Other natural products that have historically been exploited in Seychelles waters include guano and the sperm whale, which was hunted by U.S. whalers based on the island of St. Anne during the last seventy years of the nineteenth century. In recent years Seychelles has played a leading role in international movements to protect whales; in August 1981 Seychelles was declared a whale sanctuary. Since 1895, when the guano industry started, more than a million tons have been shipped from Seychelles to Mauritius, New Zealand, East Africa, Réunion, South Africa, and India. Although most of the guano is gone, there remains a lucrative trade with Mauritius, where guano is still used to fertilize sugarcane fields.

ENVIRONMENTAL DETERIORATION

In recent years, the starfish *Acanthaster*, which feeds on living coral and has done great damage to coral reefs throughout the Australia-Pacific region, has been noticed in Seychelles waters for the first time. Coral reefs are also being killed by high levels of silt that are building up from soils being carried from island streams into the sea.[16] The practice of building roadbeds or reclaiming land by using foundations of dead coral scooped from the ocean has led to widespread exploitation of coral reefs and on some occasions to the deterioration or death of living reefs. Particularly galling to many Seychellois are the ecological changes caused by the airport that have killed all life on some coral reefs and led to a silting-up of the coast.

Changes in ocean currents took place when large portions of the sea were filled to create the airport, producing a ghastly accumulation of silt and garbage on some of the shores and beaches of the northeast coast of Mahé. The government has made valiant efforts to organize garbage collection so that garbage is not dumped into the ocean in such places and in such a manner that it might destroy sea life or be washed up on shore. Most garbage, along with old cars, refrigerators, and other refuse, is presently being dumped into the sea on the other side of St. Anne Island, in the hope that a volatile and beautiful fish life might be produced in this area as a consequence of the dumping (planners have argued that such fish life has been created in the past around shipwrecks and that it should be possible to create it around deep ocean garbage dumps).

Some human diseases – like dengue fever and a number of strains of influenza – have entered the Seychelles only since the opening of the airport in 1971. Other human diseases were introduced by ship during the previous two centuries: elephantiasis, gonorrhea and other venereal diseases, hookworm, and a variety of intestinal parasites. Especially damaging to plant life, as mentioned earlier, has been the *Melittomma* beetle, which came from Madagascar. Similarly, the mynah bird has threatened a number of insect species since it was introduced from India in the 1940s, and the barn owl, from Africa, has almost caused the extinction of a few small bird species (tragically, the barn owl was purposely brought to the Seychelles to control rats but has preferred to feed on small and rare birds; attempts to control the barn owl by placing large bounties on it have often resulted in the killing of other, more valuable, owls and birds).

Perhaps even more disturbing than the introduction of disease is the obvious deterioration in the physical appearance of the islands, particularly in those areas frequented by tourists. Roadsides that were once filled with moss-covered rocks and wild flowers are now strewn with beer bottles and pop cans, candy wrappers, cigarette butts, and old plastic bags. Bits of styrofoam and patches of frothy detergent float down streams that otherwise would be among the most picturesque in the world. Almost everywhere on Mahé, it seems, one can see wrecks of old cars lying abandoned by the side of the road, stripped of their wheels, accessories, and other valuable parts, and left to rust. In contrast to an older building pattern in which even the most modest houses were spaced hundreds of yards apart, either tucked away on the sides of hilly slopes or nestled in palm groves near the beaches, crowded urban slums have now become visible in a few places. In house construction, aluminum sheeting from Australia, Japan, and India is replacing the granite and native woods and palm leaves used in older buildings. Rows of government-built houses are now trumpeted as a vast improvement on the much more distinctive shantylike structures of an earlier age.

The values of the Seychellois have undoubtedly contributed to the deterioration of their environment, especially as older values have themselves eroded. There has always been a distinct casualness about life and possessions that has led to some strewing of flotsam and jetsam about the countryside, but old-timers universally see what is happening today as deterioration. Some still remember the days a half century ago when there were only two hotels on Mahé (the Raffles and Les Palmes) and both charged a flat rate of 7 rupees a day, including meals. Victoria was then described by the Anglican Archdeacon Ozanne as a well-groomed place of "luxuriant natural growth," with a "seeming total absence of any houses whatsoever" where one "looks in vain for any town."[17] The same author described the Seychellois as follows:

> The working-class man in Seychelles may be feckless, indolent and dishonest, but he has this virtue, that he is clean in his personal habits, and he expects those about him to be clean. No matter how poor a family may be, no matter how mean their dwelling hut may be, you will always find them clean; their clothes may be, and often are, mere rags, but nevertheless, they are clean rags.

There still is a much greater sense of privacy in Seychelles than there is, for example, in India. Defecating in public is as taboo in the Seychelles as it is in Europe, although there is a custom of "going round the corner" of a tree or a big rock. The Seychellois do not like to have their pictures taken or to be stared at because they feel that the camera or stare may somehow mask the work of black magic or a gris-gris person who is trying to practice malfaisance on them. The basic cleanliness of the Seychellois is still evident from the freshly painted or freshly scrubbed look of the interior of even the poorest homes.

DEMOGRAPHIC AND ECONOMIC CHANGE

One of the most important changes that has taken place in Seychellois society in this century is the declining female-male ratio in the population. In the 1921 census women outnumbered men by 1,048 to 1,000, but by 1977 this proportion had come down to 99 women for every 100 men.[18] A relatively minor factor involved in this is the fact that the Seychelles census enumerates expatriates as well as Seychellois, and most expatriates are males. The most important reason for the declining proportion of females is an out-migration of women at a faster pace than the comparable out-migration for men, with most women going to the United States, Australia, Africa, Europe, and the Arab world. One census official estimated that something like three hundred U.S. Air Force men have married Seychellois women since the tracking station was started in 1963, a practice encouraged by the unwillingness of the U.S. government to pay moving and maintenance allowances for dependent spouses and children at the station. In recent years Seychellois women have been migrating in large numbers to Arabia and the Persian Gulf, for work as domestics and as members of harems being accumulated by wealthy Arabs.

It is occasionally argued that a second major reason for the declining proportion of women to men in Seychellois society may have something to do with the women's relatively more strenuous lives and the fact that male children are generally more highly valued than females. This is not borne out by census statistics, which indicate that females have a life expectancy at birth of 71 and males only 65. Detailed studies on the subject are unavailable, but it is clear that Seychellois women are charged with most of the responsibility for child rearing and housekeeping and that a large proportion of them also engage in employment outside the home. The fact that there is only one practicing female Seychellois doctor and one practicing female lawyer is indicative of the absence of women in higher-status positions or in professions other than teaching and nursing. As indicated earlier, the SPPF has taken significant steps to change this.

The government has been concerned about the exodus of skilled labor and professionals from the Seychelles to the point where it is now considering imposition of a substantial "guarantee to return deposit" for anyone leaving the country for a job or training abroad. Most analysts suggest that financial penalties of this kind would not affect upward out-migration curves unless they were accompanied by a healthy domestic economic situation and a more tranquil domestic political climate. In 1981 the government instituted a Rs.10,000 (US$1,600) annual fee for work permits for expatriates, with the hope that this might somehow accrue to the advantage of indigenous Seychellois. So far as anyone can tell, however, the new fee has simply been distasteful to many foreigners or has perhaps induced a few of the poorer ones to either leave or cancel plans to work in Seychelles. In almost all such cases, the position vacated by the expatriate has not been filled by a Seychellois—it has simply not been filled.

In collaboration with the International Planned Parenthood Federation, the government has moved determinedly to introduce free and widespread family planning programs into the Seychelles, including (1) establishment of family planning centers in areas of significant population; (2) free availability of the pill and other contraceptives to girls of childbearing age; (3) sex education for both boys and girls over the age of 13; and (4) free facilities for sterilizations at Victoria Hospital. For a country that is 90 percent Roman Catholic, these programs can be viewed as quite progressive, and they are responsible for the increasing (if still unsatisfactory) extent of the use of birth control measures by women in reproductive age groups. Population control advocates have recently focused on abortion as a major issue, and a liberal abortion law was pending in the People's Assembly in 1982. The present law allows abortions only for medical reasons, but the church objects even to a clause that permits an abortion for a woman who has been raped. Under these circumstances, most people suspect that the proposed liberal abortion law is doomed to defeat.

The major thrust of the government has been on social service programs for the poor and disadvantaged, partly with an eye to reducing birthrates. The theory is that a secure and healthy family is more likely to practice family planning than a poor and unhealthy one, something that has been confirmed in the aggregate by statistics collected in the past. Included in the institutions being supported by the present government are the National Council for Children, the Child Care Center, two orphanages run by the church but supported by government, the School for the Exceptional Child (meaning handicapped children), a 130-bed hospital for the handicapped, compulsory day care centers in seventeen of the Seychelles' twenty-three districts for children 4–7 years old, and a village designed to bring foster parents together with orphans in a residential atmosphere. In addition to these initiatives, the government is planning to set up voluntary day care centers for children aged 1–4 in every district.

Observers have lauded the government's intentions in promoting so many social welfare programs, but many economists have questioned the ability of the government to fully fund these programs so long as the economy continues to languish. Independent reports on the status of new social welfare programs have often been discouraging, while the continued exodus of teachers, doctors, and some of the brightest students who might serve in such programs has visibly troubled government leaders. The government has responded to large-scale outmigration by establishing or funding indigenous schools designed to provide technical training—the Management Training Center, Teachers Training Institute, Hotel School, Technical Training Institute, Ceramics Institute, Handicrafts Center, Polytechnic, and so forth—but the quality of these institutions has not been outstanding. What many fear, and what seems to be happening already, is a more or less permanent outmigration of the brightest Seychellois to other nations and the institutionalization of a set of second-rate social welfare and technical programs within Seychelles.

The poorest parts of the Seychelles are the coralline islands, which are generally sparsely populated because they lack access to fresh water. On these islands there are not enough children to maintain schools, and usually the plantation owners are the only ones wealthy enough to send

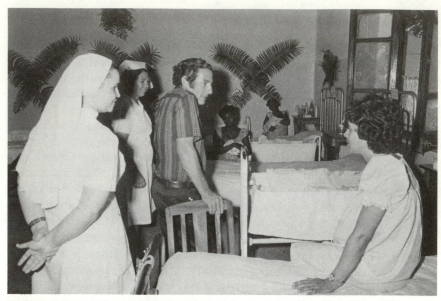

Figure 5.2. President René during a visit to a new health clinic. The major achievements of the René government have been in the areas of social welfare and services. Photo courtesy *Nation.*

their children to private primary schools on Mahé. There has been a tradition of some Seychellois working on the outer islands or abroad to send their children to one of the orphanages on Mahé, but this is not a desirable arrangement and the government is not encouraging it. In the feudalistic arrangements on the outer islands, contract laborers are invariably illiterate and the plantation manager is often called on to act as magistrate, doctor, policeman, head boatman, storekeeper, accountant, construction engineer, postman, and even priest—all simultaneously. With the modernization bent of recent governments, attempts are being made to improve the positions of the six hundred or so members of the laboring classes on the coral islands, but lack of both communications and fresh water presents serious impediments.

Immediate plans call for most new construction in the 1980s to take place on Praslin, the second largest of the Seychelles islands.[19] Both Praslin and neighboring La Digue are exquisitely beautiful places, and there is room for considerable expansion on both islands. Praslin has the attraction for tourists of being the home of the largest Coco-de-Mer forest (in the Vallée de Mai) and it also has the longest beach on any of the islands (on the "sunny side" of Praslin); La Digue has the most beautiful beach in the Seychelles, at Grand Anse. The beauty of Praslin has been somewhat impaired by the felling of large numbers of old trees in 1980 and 1981 in order to bring electricity to the island for the first time. But neither the recent loss of trees nor some minor erosion problems on Praslin should present difficulties that might inhibit planned development during the next decade. Indeed, if the government could learn from some of its mistakes on Mahé while developing Praslin in a planned manner, it could conceivably improve both the ecology of the island and the lives of its inhabitants.

La Digue, the third most populated island, presents an entirely different set of considerations from those relevant to Praslin. La Digue is an exceedingly rare place in the modern world, as it still has no electricity and no motor transport. The only industry of any consequence on La Digue is an unusual kind of tourism: Tourists come to the island by boat, ride around on bicycles or ox-carts, and see a world that still exists much as it did before the invention of electricity in the nineteenth century. The government has plans to bring electricity to La Digue via an ocean and underground network of cables, which should eliminate the need to fell large numbers of trees. However, many Seychellois (including some on La Digue) have wondered whether it might not be better for all concerned to leave the island without electricity, automobiles, and their inevitable accompaniments. More than any other place, La Digue raises fundamental moral questions about how and why the outside world should be brought to the Seychelles.

INTERNATIONAL FACTORS

One of the major difficulties in evaluating the economic and political future of the Seychelles is its ambiguous status as a very small place with heavy international responsibilities. The cost of maintaining its defense services rose from US$13.4 million in 1975 to more than US $50 million in 1981. Imports—for tourist needs and of rice and other foreign products—rose from US$44.8 million in 1976 to more than US $100 million in 1981. Although most cities or counties of only 65,000 do not have such heavy international commitments, most of them also do not have the opportunities for aid and trade present in Seychelles. During the last few years, for example, Seychelles has negotiated multimillion dollar aid or soft loan agreements with the United Kingdom, France, Belgium, Canada, the United States, China, Norway, West Germany, India, Korea, Iraq, Libya, Abu Dhabi, Kuwait, Algeria, the African Development Bank, the European Economic Community, and the World Bank. In addition, the United States is paying rent of US$2.5

Figure 5.3. President France Albert René greeting Muamar Ghadafi of Libya in 1981. Photo courtesy Seychelles Agence Press.

million per year on the tracking station, under the terms of a new contract renegotiated in 1981, which has extended the U.S. lease from 1986 to 1990.

The development strategy of the present government is to use as much aid as possible in the short run by increasing the nation's absorptive capacity and even relying on aid to meet recurring budgetary expenditures. Approximately one thousand expatriates, mostly from Europe, are resident in the Seychelles at any given time as consultants or advisers to the government or as supervisors or skilled tradesmen. Many of these foreign personnel are charged with the formulation of a variety of projects designed to attract aid donors. As the 1978–1982 Development Plan pointed out, "At present virtually 100 percent of the capital development programme is financed from foreign sources and even the recurrent budget is supplemented by aid funds."[20] The reason for such a heavy reliance on international personnel and funds is explained by the planners as follows:

> International institutions . . . with whom Seychelles is becoming increasingly involved, demand the same attention from a small country as they do from a large country. Missions from aid agencies frequently take up whole weeks of the time of key personnel. A recently independent country like Seychelles has severe problems from a shortage of professional and managerial manpower. This is overcome in the short run by the recruitment of expatriate personnel under technical cooperation arrangements, but this is not itself free of problems. It leads to high staff turnover, and frequent periods of posts being vacant. It is even the case, at times, that no suitable expatriates can be found.[21]

In the long run, of course, Seychelles would like to lessen its dependence on aid and introduce an effective program of Seychelloisation. Hopes for doing this rest partly on the development of the fishing industry and the success of oil exploration; equally important for employment and economic self-reliance are factors related to agriculture. Much of the success of self-reliance programs will depend on effective implementation of the government's ambitious social welfare and nationalization measures. Much will also depend on the outcome of Indian Ocean rivalries among the greater and lesser world powers.

Thus far, both the Soviet Union and the United States have pursued a low profile in the Seychelles, and representatives of both superpowers have exhibited a good deal of civility toward one another. But both countries have obvious interests in the islands, and both have made substantial investments relative to the small size of the country. There are 130 to 140 Americans based at the tracking station on Mahé at any given time, and some of them bring their families despite the additional costs resulting from the unwillingness of the U.S. government to pay moving costs or maintenance allowances for spouses and dependents. Those who do not have families with them live at a residential base, maintained by Pan American Airways on a subcontract with the Ford Motor Company, which has a contract with the U.S. Air Force to maintain the physical aspects of the tracking station. The tracking station is distinguished by a 100-foot (30-meter) diameter capped dome, or radome, made of 830 fiberglass panels, and by a more recently built smaller radome. These are commonly referred to as "the golfballs" because they look so much like them when viewed from a distance of 10 to 12 miles (16 to 20 kilometers) below the tracking station in Victoria.

A Seychellois adviser to the Seychelles government once described the tracking station in print as "part of an American network engaged in outer space research projects [which] receives information from a group of satellites and sends it to a central collecting point in the United States."[22] One U.S. officer in Victoria in November 1978 stated flatly that this was an inaccurate description of the station because, he claimed, the Mahé facility does not *collect* any information in Seychelles but simply "repairs and gives instructions to satellites in order to keep them in orbit and on track."[23] Much of the value of the Seychelles installation can be explained by the fact that it is the only such U.S. facility in the Southern Hemisphere and that it is almost directly opposite the headquarters of U.S. satellite technology in Sunnyvale, California. This location gives it particular significance for monitoring and commanding satellites in polar (rather than equatorial) orbit.[24] In an age of satellite spying, when two-thirds of all U.S. military messages sent abroad go via satellite, and when precise guidance for bombers, missiles, and submarines is dependent on such messages, the value of the Mahé facility is obvious.

Aside from the tracking station, the U.S. presence in Seychelles does not count for a great deal. Less than 1 percent of Seychelles exports go to the United States, and less than 2 percent of imports come from the United States.[25] The U.S. Agency for International Development (USAID) has, for the past seventeen years, funded a Food for Peace Program, administered by the Catholic Relief Services, which provides school lunches and a protein supplement prepared in government centers and is linked to the maternal and child health care projects of a variety of other charities and missionary groups. Projects that have provided assistance for brick-making and electricity, and for the establishment of agricultural research and extension services, including audiovisual materials for agriculturalists, have also been funded by USAID.

There have been more than a dozen U.S. Peace Corps volunteers in

Seychelles at any given point during the past few years, and they have assisted with everything from organization of the Carnegie Library in downtown Victoria to running a dredger in the harbor and building access roads. U.S. tourists are not yet coming in large numbers (only 2,877 came in 1980, accounting for 4 percent of the total); there is very little U.S. banking or business activity. The Bank of America does own 25 percent of one of the Victoria banks, a U.S. businessman once owned the Fisherman's Cove Hotel, and a newly planned Sheraton Hotel is to be managed by U.S. interests operating out of the Bahamas, even though it is being funded primarily by the Thapar family of India. Compared to French, British, Italian, South African, or even Indian interests on the islands, U.S. economic activity in the Seychelles is minuscule.

The U.S. community in Seychelles totals between three and four hundred people; the Soviet community is about one-third that size. The Russians have not provided economic aid or gotten involved in trade with Seychelles, but Aeroflot has opened an office in the Pirates Arms Hotel in downtown Victoria and is scheduled to begin regular flights from Moscow in 1982. Most of the Soviets on the islands have been involved in supplies of military equipment and in funding some of the political activities of the Seychelles Peoples Progressive Front (SPPF). Russians have also been conspicuous at the radio station, where TASS headquarters is located, and have provided some coaches for Seychellois sports programs. The decision by the present government to permanently terminate the services of the British Broadcasting Corporation (BBC) and to rely, almost exclusively, on its own Soviet-trained Seychelles Agence Press for news from the outside world is indicative of the extent to which the government identifies ideologically with the socialist world.

During the early years of the René regime, its most important foreign relationships were with Tanzania and the Organization of African Unity (OAU). Tanzanian "advisers" were frequently encountered in many different areas of life — in law, communications, the police and military, and in transport — and visits back and forth between Tanzanian and Seychellois officials were frequent. When Uganda and Tanzania went to war in November 1978, President René went on the radio to state that "this for us is something very serious." Admitting his dependence on Tanzanian military support, René went on to explain that the Tanzania-Uganda war "is something that we must all pay great attention to, because there is the possibility that our enemies, who very often are the same as Tanzania's, may decide that while our brothers are busy with their problems they can come and attack us."[26]

Much of the invective of the Seychelles government is reserved for the South Africans, even though South Africa provides the Seychelles with large proportions of its imports and is an enormous potential market for tourists. The government has tried to encourage imports from India, Singapore, Australia, and Europe, but thus far no one can compete with the South Africans, except in the fields of automobile manufacturing and electronics, where the Japanese have cornered the Seychelles market. The quality of Indian goods tends to be inferior to that of South African products, and Indian shipping to the Seychelles is sporadic at best. Singapore, Australia, and European countries find it difficult to undersell the South Africans or to supply goods as frequently and as dependably. Ships from elsewhere are infrequent and irregular; in contrast, the South Africans send a ship to Seychelles every week. One Seychellois merchant explained his preference for importing from South Africa as follows:

> If I telephone Durban an hour before that ship leaves, my goods are on the ship and delivered in Victoria a few days later. If there is something wrong with the goods, they are replaced with no questions asked. The goods are of uniformly high quality and usually sell for much less than elsewhere. I can't get that kind of service anywhere else in the world.[27]

The Seychelles government has enthusiastically joined the OAU and the African "front-line" states in votes designed to impose trade boycotts and protectionist tariffs against South Africa, but severe difficulties in implementing these resolutions have resulted from the inability or unwillingness of anyone to subsidize such measures. In the meantime, the dependence of Seychelles on South Africa, like the dependence of Mauritius and other African nations, has been increasing steadily with each passing year. President René has indicated on a number of occasions that he does not like the situation, but thus far his government has been ineffectual in changing it. Representative of René's ambiguity on this score was a speech he made in October 1977, in which he said:

> In the past we have depended very much on South Africa. We don't think this is a very good thing. We are doing what we can to change this dependency. As for South African tourists, it's a different matter. They are welcome. But if they think that by coming on holiday in Seychelles they are supporting a system to which they are opposed, it's up to them to decide.[28]

Relations with both Britain and France have been strained since the René government came to power, with the result that British aid has been leveling off and French aid was at one point dropped entirely. The great rupture in France's relations with the Seychelles occurred in December 1979 when the René government accused the French of collaborating with people in the Seychelles to stage a coup. According to the Seychelles government version, two French technical consultants (called *coopérants* by French officials) to the Seychelles police force were conspiring with French *coopérants* assigned to help run the Seychelles' only naval vessel, a minesweeper that France had previously given to Seychelles for use in patrolling the islands. The Seychelles government declared two French diplomats, the two French *coopérants* in the police force, and six French *coopérants* on the naval vessel persona non grata and arrested 120 Seychellois who were suspected of involvement in the plot. The French responded by withdrawing six other *coopérants* and suspending all aid programs. By March 1980 the French had begun to replace some of the people who had been withdrawn, aid programs were slowly resumed, and relations began to improve. With the election of socialist François Mitterrand as president of France in June 1981, relations with the Seychelles were expected to return to normal.

The 1979–1980 rift in relations with France dramatized the insecurity of the René regime in its dealings with foreign governments. Having come to power in a coup supported by Tanzania, René has been highly conscious of the need to structure his own foreign policy in such a way as to prevent his enemies from conspiring with outside powers against him. René's official policy is one of nonalignment, with the vast bulk of Seychelles' economic ties being oriented to the West and almost all of its political ties to the socialist bloc.[29] René's public political commitment to the Soviets can be gauged by the way in which official bookstores and public libraries are flooded with Soviet, North Korean, and Cuban propaganda, while literature from the United States and Europe is censored and sometimes banned. It is also indicated by Seychelles' enthusiastic support of Soviet actions on all international issues, including the most ringing verbal endorsement by any nation of the Soviet invasion of Afghanistan.

Some observers have speculated that the Soviet Union might be using Seychelles as an arms cache for future supply of stockpiled arms to revolutionaries on other islands in the Indian Ocean and the East African coast. Prime Minister Seewoosagur Ramgoolam of Mauritius has been so concerned on this score that he has inititated strict security checks on all vessels coming to Mauritius from Seychelles and has tried to build relationships with South Africa and the United States.[30] René's regime has responded by openly supporting the socialist opposition in Mauritius (the Movement Militant Mauritian, led by Paul Berenger) while moving closer to already established revolutionary socialist regimes in the Malagasy Republic and Mozambique.

Most Seychellois Foreign Ministry officials argue that their present posture of nonalignment is essential, and they also see it as having fairly good chances of success in preserving the country's independence. Under the present circumstances, to take the extreme case, were the Soviets to attempt a takeover in the Seychelles, they would find it extremely difficult to run the economy because the tourist industry would almost certainly collapse and essential imports from South Africa would be cut off. On the other hand, were the Americans or Europeans to intervene in Seychelles politics, the present regime could close down or create difficulties in the operation of the satellite tracking station and could use the Soviets to escalate the level of political rhetoric to a fever pitch. In this atmosphere, it is perhaps not surprising that the SPPF contains both pro-American and pro-Russian factions, with most party leaders striving for a balance between the superpowers. Thus far the factional balance has been so delicate that intraparty proposals for anti-American demonstrations have always been met by proposals for anti-Soviet demonstrations; the consequence is that party demonstrations against either of the superpowers have not yet taken place.

CONCLUSIONS

When assessing the future prospects of the Seychelles, it is important to remember that the islands, although important, are not at the central focus of concern for any of the nations involved in Indian Ocean diplomacy (Figure 5.4). The USSR has expanded its naval capability in the Indian Ocean since 1968 to the point where it recently had twenty-one ships there, but most of its attention has been given to the installation of naval facilities (including submarine pens and missile repair and storage silos) for its exclusive use on the island of Socotra (in the Arabian Sea), on Perim and the Dahlak Archipelago (islands belonging to South Yemen and Ethiopia, respectively, in the Red Sea), at the old British port of Aden in Southern Yemen, and at Cam Ranh Bay in Vietnam.[31] The United States — which has recently had thirty-two combat and support vessels in the Indian Ocean — has committed hundreds of millions of dollars for the improvement of its naval facilities in the Kenyan port of Mombasa, Berbera in Somalia, Egypt's Ras Banas, several bases in Oman, and the major U.S. naval station on the island of Diego Garcia in the Chagos Archipelago.[32] Since the Soviet invasion of Afghanistan, Russian jets can now reach the crucial Strait of Hormuz (through which much of the world's oil flows) from Kandahar in less than an hour. President Ronald Reagan has responded with resumption of multibillion-dollar military aid to Pakistan, including the sale of advanced F-16 fighters, and a massive naval buildup in the Indian Ocean. Some idea of the importance of the ocean to the United States can be gained from the fact that sixty-nine of seventy-two strategic raw materials imported by

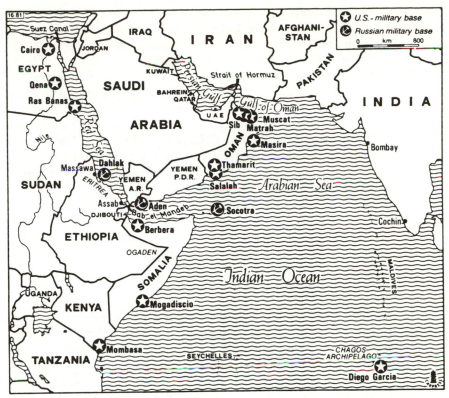

Figure 5.4. Naval bases in the Indian Ocean. From *The Hindu* (newspaper in Madras, India), March 5, 1981. Published with permission.

the United States are found in the thirty-six countries on the Indian Ocean littoral.[33]

The Soviets have in the past tried to acquire the naval base at Diégo-Suarez on Madagascar, which the French abandoned after Madagascar achieved its independence.[34] Similarly, the Soviets negotiated unsuccessfully for the old abandoned British naval base at Gan, in the Maldives. A major objective of the Soviet Union in the Indian Ocean has been support of African liberation movements willing to challenge South Africa's white minority government, as demonstrated by the Soviet willingness to send three warships to the port of Maputo in Mozambique in mid-1981 after a South African raid into that country. Soviet warships have called at times at ports in India, Sri Lanka, Mauritius, and Seychelles, where limited services are available to them. India and Sri Lanka have specifically barred all foreign ships carrying nuclear weapons.

Prior to 1977, both the United States and USSR had shown considerable restraint in the Indian Ocean, but Soviet willingness to send Cuban troops to Ethiopia and other African states in 1977, together with its subsequent invasion of Afghanistan and the fall of the shah of Iran, led the United States to escalate the level of its naval capabilities, to create a 60,000-strong Rapid Deployment Force that could be used to mobilize troops within seventy-two hours for action in the Gulf, and to adopt the so-called Carter Doctrine, which commits the United States to military action in the Gulf in the event of Soviet aggression.[35] The Soviets contend that they have no intention of invading or subverting the countries on the littoral of the ocean, but are instead seeking three objectives: (1) to secure Soviet maritime and fishing areas in order to protect their own warm-water naval traffic between Vladivostok and the Black Sea; (2) to support African liberation movements directed against South Africa; and (3) to counteract U.S. missile-carrying submarines that could stage attacks on the Soviet Union from the Indian Ocean region. Independent observers have also suggested that the Soviets have a major interest in the mineral resources of Southern Africa and the Indian Ocean seabed.

Countries on the littoral of the ocean are divided into two groups, which are generally considered to be pro- and anti-Soviet.[36] The pro-Soviet nations, led by India, advocate a "zone of peace" concept and confine their criticism of the superpowers to the United States. The anti-Soviet nations, led by Pakistan and the countries of the Association of Southeast Asian Nations (ASEAN), call for a "balanced presence" and openly express fears of Soviet aggression.

None of the countries on the littoral of the Indian Ocean has the military capability to repel the superpowers.[37] India has the largest navy of any of the littoral nations (47,000 men). Its firepower consists of one aged aircraft carrier, two old cruisers, eight outdated submarines, twenty-eight frigates (of which eight are modern), a dozen corvettes and missile boats, the usual complement of minesweepers and landing craft, and fifty naval planes. Naval authorities consider the Indian navy quite inadequate to patrol its own 3,600-mile (6,000-kilometer) coastline, which has 10 major ports and 300 minor ports, an extended economic maritime zone, and oilfields offshore from Bombay. Granted its insufficiencies for patrolling its own waters, it is little wonder that the Indian navy has resisted invitations to provide cooperative assistance to nations like Seychelles.

In a world besieged by big power rivalries for increasingly scarce resources, a small country like Seychelles has very few options. As Burton Benedict has pointed out, it could become a military base for one or another of the big powers, but this would probably make it more vulnerable than it is already.[38] Had things worked out differently for Mancham, it might have become a convenience to the powers, as Hong Kong is to China and the West. In the event, it has chosen nonalignment and maneuvering between the powers, causing itself numerous problems that result primarily from the conflict between jet-set tourism and Marxist economics.

Over the years the Seychelles have been painted as a highly romantic place. The praise of nineteenth-century visitors like Charles Darwin, H. M. Stanley, and Charles "Chinese" Gordon of Khartoum has been echoed in the twentieth century by writers like Henry de Monfried and other visitors like Bing Crosby, the Duke of Edinburgh, and Queen Elizabeth. A number of recent novels that have been set in the Seychelles—Compton MacKenzie's *Mezzotint,* Ian Fleming's *Hildebrand's Rarity,* or Claire Lorrimer's *Chantal*—have added to the aura of intrigue and mystery that is often associated with the islands.

Nostalgia was intensified by the regime of "Jimmy" Mancham, who was the kind of person who would spontaneously pop into shops to say hello to people or walk down the street greeting people for a few hours every day he was in the Seychelles. One morning when the people who ran the radio station overslept, Mancham himself went over and opened it up by acting as disc jockey for a few hours. People still talk about the year that Mancham announced the arrival of Father Christmas on an Air France flight from Paris and then went out to the airport himself to play the role of Santa Claus. In sharp contrast to Mancham's colorful years in power, the René regime has been drab and businesslike. René himself does not mix easily with people, he keeps himself aloof, and he is increasingly shielded behind heavy security. Christmas is now a dreary affair, public drinking and merriment having been disallowed.

Recent tourist promotions in Europe and the United States have advertised the Seychelles as "a place to get the dust off," with high-priced packaged tours featuring a week or two at game parks in East Africa and a week or two on the beaches of Mahé, Praslin, or LaDigue. To the tourist, the Seychelles do offer as attractive a combination of sights and activities as one could imagine: paragliding, windsurfing and water skiing, snorkeling and scuba-diving, deep-sea fishing and yachting; an incomparable opportunity to view sea life, shells, and plants in their natural setting; and a clean and stimulating environment of dancing, music, museums, good restaurants, and curiosities. Seychelles is still so undeveloped that it was possible just a few years ago for a Britisher wanting to emulate Robinson Crusoe to spend almost a year on an uninhabited island without being noticed.[39]

But there are many conflicts to be resolved in the Seychelles before the great tourism potential of the islands can be realized. Moreover, in the final analysis, the Seychelles government may not have all that much to say about the future of the islands. It will have to make some attempts to move in the direction of its populist rhetoric, but it is simply too dependent on foreign investment and the skills of the indigenous elite to effect a radical restructuring of society. Armed intervention from outside could conceivably happen again, but observers are universally agreed that the next such intervention would inevitably produce bloodshed and would most likely exacerbate tensions to such an extent that an irretrievable instability might be created. Unfortunately, the best alternative for the Seychelles might well be the tenuous kind of arrangement it has at present, with foreign influence being confined largely to behind-the-scenes maneuvers that do nothing more than contribute to the mystery and romance, and ultimately to the despoliation, of this most beautiful of places.

NOTES

1. Quoted from B. G. Verghese, *Halfway to Everywhere: The Seychelles, Indian Ocean Republic* (New Delhi: Commerce Pamphlet No. 105, 1976), p. 7.
2. The campaign is described in Tony Beamish, *Aldabra Alone* (London: Allen and Unwin, 1970), pp. 30ff.
3. Professor Stoddart, who has studied the Seychelles for more than three decades, is in the process of completing a book, entitled *A Biogeography of Seychelles*, to be published in Holland in 1982.
4. The work of the people on Cousin Island is described in *Cousin Island: Nature Reserve* (Victoria: International Council for Bird Preservation, 1981).
5. See Malcolm Penny, *The Birds of Seychelles and the Outlying Islands* (London: William Collins Sons and Company, 1974).
6. An excellent short discussion of Seychelles wildlife is provided in Jeremy High, *The Natural History of the Seychelles* (London: G. T. Phillips and Company, 1976).
7. A bibliography is provided in Guy Lionnet, *The Romance of a Palm: Coco-de-Mer*, 4th ed. (Victoria: Imprimerie St. Fidel, 1978), p. 41.
8. The original manuscript was entitled *Eden and Its Two Sacramental Trees*. It was reprinted under the title "Seychelles and the Garden of Eden," in *Palestine Exploration Fund Quarterly* (April 1885), pp. 78ff.
9. Julian Mockford, *Pursuit of an Island* (New York: Staples Press, 1950), p. 133.
10. See John Proctor, *Conservation in the Seychelles: Report of the Conservation Adviser, 1970* (Victoria: Government Printers, 1970).
11. See C. J. Piggott, *A Report on a Visit to the Outer Islands of Seychelles* (Tolworth, Surrey: Land Resources Division, Directorate of Overseas Surveys, 1969).
12. The official conservation policy of the Seychelles is laid down in a

White Paper, entitled *Conservation Policy in the Seychelles* (Victoria: Government of Seychelles, 1971).

13. Jourdain's descriptions of the natural life of the Seychelles are discussed in Guy Lionnet, *A Short History of the Seychelles* (Victoria: Imprimerie St. Fidel, 1974), pp. 21ff.

14. Beamish, *Aldabra Alone*, p. 160.

15. Ibid., pp. 96–97.

16. The coral reef environment is described in N.V.C. Polunin and F.R.J. Williams, *Coral Reef Fish of Seychelles* (Hong Kong: Government Printer, 1979), pp. 8ff.

17. J.A.F. Ozanne, *Coconuts and Creoles* (London: Philip Allan and Company, 1936), pp. 21, 90.

18. Republic of Seychelles, *1977 Census Report* (Victoria: Government of Seychelles, 1978), p. 45.

19. The basic plan document, now somewhat out of date, is *Seychelles Structure Plan, 1975* (Victoria: Government Printers, 1974).

20. Republic of Seychelles, *National Development Plan, 1978–1982* (Victoria: Government Printers, 1978), p. 16.

21. Ibid., p. 21.

22. Guy Lionnet, *The Seychelles* (Harrisburg, Pa.: Stackpole Books, 1972), pp. 156–157.

23. Quoted from an interview in November 1978.

24. See E. E. Lasch, "Satellite Tracking in Seychelles," *Journal of the Seychelles Society*, No. 3 (December 1963), pp. 28–32; and "The Colony of the Seychelles," in *Area Handbook for the Indian Ocean Territories*, edited by Theodore L. Stoddard et al. (Washington, D.C.: Government Printing Office, 1973), pp. 55–74.

25. Republic of Seychelles, *Statistical Bulletin, Fourth Quarter, 1980*, Vol. 1, no. 3 (February 1981), pp. 17–21.

26. *Nation* (Victoria daily), November 6, 1978, p. 1.

27. Quoted from an interview in August 1981.

28. Quoted in *Weekend Life* (Victoria weekly), Vol. 1, no. 15 (October 8, 1977), p. 8.

29. The basic document outlining Seychelles' official foreign policy is France Albert René, *Seychelles' Stand on World Affairs* (Victoria: Ministry of Education and Information, 1979).

30. Ramgoolam is strongly opposed to apartheid and has condemned the U.S. base on Diego Garcia, but he has broken ranks with his militant neighbors by allowing South African Airways transit rights in Mauritius, initiating regular flights by Air Mauritius to South Africa, and refusing to press very hard the Mauritian legal claim to Diego Garcia. See Deepak Razdan, "Mauritius Looking More to South Africa," *Hindustan Times* (New Delhi), July 19, 1981, p. 3.

31. This section on Indian Ocean diplomacy is heavily dependent on an excellent series of three articles by Michael T. Kaufman in the *New York Times*, April 19, 20, 21, 1981.

32. A description of the U.S. naval base at Diego Garcia by one of the few

journalists who has been allowed to travel there is Jack Fuller, "Dateline Diego Garcia: Paved-Over Paradise," *Foreign Policy*, No. 28 (Fall 1977), pp. 175–186.

33. "The New Heart of the World: The Indian Ocean," *The Hindu* (Madras), March 5, 1981, p. 6. This article was translated and reprinted from the original in *Le Monde* (Paris).

34. An excellent collection of articles on the strategic environment of the Indian Ocean appears in *The Indian Ocean in Global Politics*, edited by Larry W. Bowman and Ian Clark (Boulder, Colo.: Westview Press, 1980).

35. U.S. policy in the Indian Ocean is analyzed by Monoranjan Bezboruah, *U.S. Strategy in The Indian Ocean: The International Response* (New York: Praeger Publishers, 1977).

36. See K. P. Misra, *Quest for an International Order in the Indian Ocean* (Bombay: Allied Publishers, 1977), esp. pp. 65ff.

37. V. K. Bhasin, *Super Power Rivalry in the Indian Ocean* (New Delhi: S. Chand and Company, 1981), pp. 127ff.

38. Burton Benedict, *Problems of Smaller Territories* (London: Athlone Press for the Institute of Commonwealth Studies, University of London, 1967), p. 9.

39. The experience has been recounted in Macdonald Hastings, *After You, Robinson Crusoe* (London: Pelham Publishers, 1975).

Selected Bibliography

Benedict, Burton. *People of the Seychelles*. 3rd ed. Ministry of Overseas Development, Overseas Research Publication No. 14. London: Her Majesty's Stationery Office, 1970.

Employment and Poverty in the Seychelles: Report of a Study Organised by the Institute of Development Studies, Percy Selwyn, Chairman. Brighton: University of Sussex, 1980.

Fayon, Maxime. *Geography of Seychelles*. 2nd rev. ed. Victoria: Ministry of Education and Culture, 1978.

Lee, Christopher. *Seychelles: Political Castaways*. London: Hamish Hamilton, 1976.

Lionnet, Guy. *The Seychelles*. Harrisburg, Pa.: Stackpole Books, 1972.

Ostheimer, John M. "Independence Politics in the Seychelles." In *The Politics of the Western Indian Ocean Islands*, edited by John M. Ostheimer (New York: Praeger Publishers, 1975), pp. 161–192.

Ozanne, J.A.F. *Coconuts and Creoles*. London: Philip Allan and Company, 1936.

Sauer, Jonathan. *Plants and Man on the Seychelles Coast: A Study in Historical Biogeography* (Madison: University of Wisconsin Press, 1967).

Seychelles: Economic Memorandum. Report Prepared by Robert Maubouche and Naimeh Hadjitarkhani. Washington, D.C.: Eastern Africa Regional Office, World Bank, 1980.

Shah, Kantilal Jivan. "Fragments of History." *Commerce* (Bombay), Special Independence of Seychelles Issue, Vol. 132, no. 3396 (June 26, 1976):9–32.

Thomas, Athol. *Forgotten Eden: A View of the Seychelles Islands in the Indian Ocean*. London: Orient Longmans, 1969.

Veevers-Carter, Wendy Day. *Island Home*. New York: Random House, 1970.

Webb, A.W.T. *Story of Seychelles*. 3rd rev. ed. Victoria: Government Printing Office, 1966.

Index